Praise for Intuitive

Speaking through the voice of the Tri Luminii and her own, Nicole delivers guidance and wisdom for connecting to and accepting our intuition. She teaches us how to more fully experience the world from a place of unconditional love. A read that is both exhilarating and calming.

> — Connie Jo Miller, Owner,
> Enigma Bookkeeping Solutions

Have you been working to increase your intuition? Then *Intuitive Languages: Your Field Guide to Live in Alignment and Flow* is a must-read! This step-by-step (clair-by-clair) guide brings enormous clarity and simplicity to your journey with incredible results. I felt my intuition perk up just by reading the book! But it has an even greater purpose, which I fell in love with! The Tri Luminii's uplifting vision for our planet, channeled through Nicole Meltzer, is based on Unconditional Love. By showing us how to get into the Flow of Life through reconnecting with all the planet's sentient beings, the Tri Luminii provided me with hope for our world.

> — Maribeth Decker, animal communicator and
> bestselling author of *Peace in Passing: Comfort for
> Loving Human Beings During Animal Transitions*

In her book, *Intuitive Languages*, author Nicole Meltzer together with the Tri Luminii take you on a fascinating journey into understanding and activating your intuition. I really enjoyed the simple exercises that help you discover how you experience your intuition and how to strengthen it. For anyone wishing to better understand and employ their intuition, this book is a valuable guide.

— Cheri D. Andrews, Esq., author of
*Smooth Sailing: A Practical Guide to
Legally Protecting Your Business*

It's something we all have access to but may not fully trust in ourselves: Intuition. Nicole and the Tri Luminii share beautifully and with great clarity, how to identify our individual way of knowing, cultivating receptivity and guidance with ease. A practical and informative experiential guidebook, *Intuitive Languages* will help you build that trust in your capacity to access and activate your intuition intentionally. It is a must-read for anyone interested in living intuitively, from the person who identifies as highly intuitive to the person just beginning to explore the concept of intuition. Give yourself this gift and you will be bathed in unconditional love and support simply through the reading of this book, growing your awareness and trust in your experience and intuitive knowing in the process.

— Becca Weinstein, intuitive visionary and artist,
InnerFire Visioning for Empowered Alignment

In an increasingly divided and disconnected world, Intuitive Languages is salve for the soul. The focus on our interconnectedness, not only to each other, but also to Source, is profoundly calming and grounding. It is a joy to read and I look forward to employing the practices discussed! A beautiful guide for those longing to reconnect to themselves and all that is seen and unseen around them.

— Nicolette Blanco, author of *By a Thread: Resilience Strategies for the Partially Unraveled*

If you have been struggling to notice and understand messages for you from the Universe, this is the book for you. *Intuitive Languages* is a very practical guide that steps you through a logical process to expand your intuition and make those messages available to you. I have worked with Nicole for years and her process is doable and effective. Read this book and add a little flow to your life!

— Judy Kane, founder of Aligned Consciousness and author of *Your4Truths: How Beliefs Impact Your Life*

As someone who has vivid, lucid dreams, I often wondered why I was having them. Am I going a little crazy, or is The Universe trying to tell me something? Thanks to *Intuitive Languages* by Nicole Meltzer, I now know the answer: My dreams are part of my intuitive process. *Intuitive Languages* is your guidebook to receiving and understanding what Source is trying to tell you - whether through metaphors you see while meditating, to sensation you receive seemingly from nowhere. Every day and in every way, you are receiving spiritual guidance. With *Intuitive Languages* at your disposal, you'll now be able to understand these messages, helping you live a more fulfilled, aligned life.

— Jill Celeste, MA, author, *Loud Woman: Good-bye, Inner Good Girl*

Intuitive Languages is a must-read for anyone seeking to understand their connection to Spirit. It enlightens readers on the various ways our intuition may appear and how to connect to it. Spiritual seekers will love this book!

— Suzanne Tregenza Moore, author, *Hang on Tight!: Learn to Love the Roller Coaster of Entrepreneurship*

Intuitive Languages

Intuitive Languages

*Your Field Guide to Live
in Alignment and Flow*

Nicole Meltzer

Edited by
Deborah Kevin

HIGHLANDER
PRESS

ISBN: 978-1-956442-09-0
Ebook ISBN: 978-1-956442-10-6
Library of Congress Control Number: 2022945112

Published by Highlander Press
501 W. University Pkwy, Ste. B2
Baltimore, MD 21210

Cover artwork: Jenny Giles
Cover layout: Patricia Creedon
Editor: Deborah Kevin
Author photo: Victoria Dietz

This book is dedicated to your intuitive awakening. Whether you're on the first step of your journey or have been walking this path for decades, or somewhere in-between, may the words and energies imprinted in this book bring you a deeper connection to your intuition.

Contents

About the Cover

When I first envisioned what the cover of this book would look like, I had a million ideas for the direction we could pursue. What I knew for sure was there needed to be a tree. Trees hold a special place in my heart. As a child, I gravitated towards the trees for comfort, calmness and adventure. The most special tree was the one at my grandmother's home. I spent a lot of time with her. She lived in a one-level apartment complex which was set up like a court. All of the living rooms of the apartments faced the courtyard. And in that courtyard stood a majestic crimson maple tree. Under her canopy, the "ladies of the court" met and discussed the goings-on of the day. The majority of the ladies were retired and I became the unofficial granddaughter for each of them. I loved listening to their stories and daydreamed about the places they had come from and what life must've been like for them when they were my age. This place, under the tree, was a magical spot for me.

Trees play a significant role in the teachings of my ancestors, the Celts. For the ancient Celts, trees were the keepers of the wisdom. Their roots connect us to the Earth's energy and wisdom. Their canopies connect us to the heavens' energy and wisdom. Trees live long lives and bear witness to many generations, and the wisdom of the people surrounding them. I resonate deeply with this energy teaching.

Once we had the concept of having a tree be the focal point of the cover, we met with a few artists to gather their ideas. I have to say, the process was a lot of fun. I love art, and to see interpretations of your work, in art form, is a trippy experience! I knew something special was coming though, when I received an email from Debby (CEO of Highlander Press) telling me about an artist with whom she knew I would be aligned: Jenny Giles. She is a creative superstar in Wales, UK, and she knows how to see into my soul! I had briefly explained the process for intuitive meditation which I teach to my Flow members. Loosely speaking, it involves a scavenger hunt for metaphoric Easter eggs from Spirit. I was floored when I saw the concept art Jenny put together. I have never been able to describe what I experience, visually, in a meditation. I don't know how she was able to grab it and bring into reality, but I am so thankful she did.

I gave Jenny a list of the most common objects my Flow members perceive within their meditations. From this list she created a mystical scene of messages ready to be received. Would you like to receive a message now? To begin, make an intention for guidance. You can ask a specific questions or you can ask for a general message. Now relax your eyes and allow an object to grab your attention. The ask yourself, "What does a ____ mean to me?" Let's say, for example, the fox is the object you focused on. Here are some questions to ask yourself. What does a fox mean to you? What makes a fox different from a coyote? What are you reminded of when you see a fox? This is your translation, message, or answer to your question.

How to Use This Book

THE CORE OF THIS BOOK IS WRITTEN AS A DIRECT CHANNEL OF the Tri Luminii. Their way of speaking and communicating can feel structurally awkward to the well-versed in English grammar. There is always a reason, energetically, behind the way they communicate. For this reason, I encourage you to feel into the words, as you read them. Allow yourself to be immersed in their energy, knowing that if you don't "get it" on a conscious level, unconsciously you are understanding and processing the information. In fact, even if you do "get it", know that you are processing the message on a deeper level unconsciously! Their way of communication is multi-layered, and you will get something deeper, each time you experience their words.

The structure of building your Intuitive Language is their wisdom and offering. They have laid out the information in a way that builds upon itself. Fight the urge to jump to the section to which you are initially drawn. As you build your Intuitive Language, you will see why it has been mapped out the way it is shown here.

I have also added my experience as a life-long intuitive and teacher of intuition. To avoid confusion, I have clearly indicated where I am adding in guidance and stories to help you process and assimilate the guidance from the Tri Luminii. It has been my experience that witnessing others' journeys in intuition offers a deeper understanding of one's own intuitive journey. I have pulled stories from my own journey, and from the journey of my students. Find yourself in these stories.

Building your Intuitive Language is not a passive experience. I encourage you to keep a journal handy as you go through the book. The Tri Luminii have offered some exercises and reflective thoughts throughout the book. There is also a free workbook to accompany you on this journey in building your Intuitive Language. You can download it at: www.NicoleMeltzer.com

Finally, the most important element in building your Intuitive Language is in having fun! Although you can create some really amazing things in your life as a result of developing your intuition, and you can make a significant impact on the world, it is imperative to remain in a curious and playful energy. If this is your first exposure to the Tri Luminii, prepare to be delighted!

Message from Nicole

As I write these words, the world is in lockdown. The fear in the collective is palpable. In this fear comes judgement, scapegoatism, us/them mentality, segregation and frustration. We are frustrated as a society for so many reasons. Long-held ideologies and social structures are ready to be taken down, if not transformed. The energy is heavy. It is thick. And as an empathetic intuitive, I am feeling it all! I have days when I just want to stay in bed and shut the world out. I know I'm not the only one. Perhaps you've been experiencing this as well. So, why write a book in such a challenging time? In short, because I believe whole-heartedly that if we are going to progress as a species into a place of love and compassion, we need to tune into our intuition. And more truthfully, the Tri Luminii won't leave me alone until I do!

Being an intuitive is the part of me I kept hidden for years. Fear of rejection and ridicule kept me from standing fully in my power and, regretfully, from helping more people. In fact, the very part of me which I avoided sharing was actually my greatest asset to share. Being intuitive has helped me direct one-to-one sessions with my clients in the direction that brought the greatest healing and transformation. In classes it has helped me use "just the right words" that will transform and resonate deeply with each student who needs the information in order to achieve their a-ha moment. And for me personally, it has helped make the healing and growing process much easier and gentler.

Twenty years ago, when I first began my journey of formally honing my intuitive skills, my teacher intuited I would, one day, trance channel a collective of energies which would create a great shift of awareness and provide an opening of connection for humans. You know, no biggie! ;) I was a master at hiding and keeping myself small, so really, this was a big stretch and admittedly, I brushed it off. The thought of trance channeling scared me. I didn't like the idea of letting Spirit into my body and taking over communication. It was probably a result of watching too many horror films in my younger years! Thankfully, I was blessed with years of training with Spirit communication and was held lovingly by my own guides throughout the process. However, when Spirit wants to speak with you, it will find a way! And when it was time, the Tri Luminii arrived.

I was first introduced to the Tri Luminii when I was vacationing with my family in the Caribbean. I sat on the balcony of our state-room on the cruise ship, enjoying the beauty of the early morning sunrise at sea. There, in my robe and a coffee in hand, I became acutely aware of a strong presence beside me. It's not unusual for me to tune into energies, so it didn't startle me. However, I admit, I was annoyed. I didn't want to be in communication with any spirits or to have to "work". I just wanted to enjoy the sunrise! Everyone was still asleep, and I had these precious moments to myself. I think any parent of young children can relate to that feeling! The energy must have picked up on my annoyance because they patiently waited for the sun to break past the horizon before speaking with me. I felt a rising feeling of love as their presence became stronger. The love was so strong, I burst into tears. I had never felt such a peaceful, loving and expansive feeling as this before. As the love grew inside of me, they presented themselves as three beams of light.

"Greetings our loved one, we are the Tri Luminii."

These simple words began what would become a beautiful relationship of love, growth and insight.

They are not the first collective of energies I have trance channelled. There have been others before them. I have found the process of trancing them to be quite different, though. I don't know if it is that we are better aligned on our energies; or if their focus on unconditional love is also a consistent driving force in my life; or just simply I've grown in my abilities. Whatever the reason, I have deep gratitude for our connection and for the opportunity to introduce you to the Tri Luminii, their messages of unconditional love, and their guidance in helping us all decipher our Intuitive Languages.

This is the first time I have written while trance channeling. The words within this book are the translation of the energies and wisdom shared by the Tri Luminii through my filter. It is important to remember, any time you listen to a channel, there is a process of filtration which happens. Spirit uses the words of the human channeling. There is a matching up process of vibrations. All words hold their own vibration, and as the channel comes through, it must find the matching vibration. For this reason, the expressions can come through clunky at times. My advice is to feel into the words and find your own interpretation.

As you read this book, I encourage you to feel their loving presence with you. In a world that can seem in lack of love at times, the

Tri Luminii offer us that which we have been craving in our being. Love and connection - without conditions. Each word they communicate is delivered in this love energy. Just gazing upon the words, you will be able to feel it.

Thank you for choosing this journey with us. Please know that, whether we meet in person, or not, I love you deeply.

Meet the Tri Luminii

Greetings Loved Ones. We are the Tri Luminii. We are communicating with you at this moment in your evolution to assist in the opening of Love and connection between all living beings on your beautiful planet, and beyond. You are ready. You are eager. You are aching for loving connection. We feel this and wish to be of assistance.

Our message is not one of Galactic wars nor movement through dimensions. Our message is of Unconditional Love. This is the energy from which all beings come, and to where all beings will return. It is the vibration which unlocks and accesses Universal wisdom. It is the current of communication between realms. Ours is a unifying message. As we experience it, when humans are connected to Unconditional Love, they are operating from their highest, truest Self. They are in co-creation with the Universe and with each other. There is no need for controlling another when you are connected, because you will experience that all you need is available to you constantly. Additionally, when connected to this energy and being in this state, others cannot control you. This is the ultimate experience of self-empowerment. This is not without conflict and contrast.

Conflict and contrast is experienced differently, however. It is more collaborative.

The journey of the Unconditional Love Movement begins with identifying and living your Intuitive Language. There are three steps to this process. The first is preparing to receive. The second is being in a state of receiving. The third is the mode of receiving.

Our intention is for this process to be a fun, playful, and inspiring one for you. As Nicole mentioned, we have infused the Unconditional Love energy in every word we communicate to you. Presence yourself to it. See, how you become increasingly aware of our presence with you as you embark on this journey.

Always know, we love you, unconditionally.

Connection to Love

Your state of being. The way you go about your day. The emotional energy you carry. These are the strong determinants in how well you will perceive, and ultimately, acknowledge, the guidance you are constantly receiving. Please hear this. There is never a moment when messages and guidance are not being given to you. You are supported. You are loved. Always.

An integral step in building your Intuitive Language is bringing yourself into a state of being that opens the channel to become aware of the receiving. For this, we ask you to become aware of your connection to unconditional love. Unconditional love is our favourite topic to discuss. It is the energy from which we all derive. It is the most natural energy to be in. When you experience unconditional love, whether giving or receiving, you awaken to your True Self. You awaken to your connection to all there is and eliminate the perception of barriers and boundaries between you and all living things. It is in this state, you are most receptive to receiving, because there is no separation. You are aware of the wisdom of the Universe. You are the wisdom of the Universe. And, as we have observed you and your dance with unconditional love, we know it takes practice!

Feeling unconditional love is a stretch for many people. It's not because you are incapable of conjuring it up, it is because unconditional love has been perceived as a big conceptual energy. It is also perceived as a far-off goal of fairytale romances. We are not speaking of romance here. Unconditional love is beyond romance. This is because romance is experienced between two separated beings. When you are in a state of unconditional love, there is no separation. And you can most definitely experience this way of being in your romantic relationships, too.

How does one experience love unconditionally, when you live in a realm of duality? Your very existence and your relation to all things around you are based on conditions. How do you know who or what you are, without the comparison of yourself to others? Please know, we are not talking about comparisons in a good and bad, better or worse, way. What we speak of is, you know you are you, because you are not anyone else. You are your own unique expression of unconditional love and this is the beautiful aspect of incarnating on Earth, in a dualistic reality, where you get to experience this differentiation. The challenge comes when you spend too much time in the duality. This will begin to look like judgement, segregation, "us and them" mentality, hierarchies and cliques. The respites of experiencing unconditional love, allow you to refuel, reconnect, and recalibrate your vibration and energy levels. We believe you would benefit from creating a routine or habit of taking regular breaks to connect to unconditional love, just as you would grab a glass of water, get sufficient sleep and eat regularly. We feel it is vital to a well-lived life.

We are aware that connecting to unconditional love may not be a switch easy to flip on. We would like to help you with this. There are emotions, feelings and ways of being which serve as amplifiers and igniters for unconditional love. The key to finding your ignition is to examine when you have felt an unconditional love connection. We have some reflection questions to offer you:

1. When was the last time you felt connected to all there is - when you felt the expansiveness of living beyond your physical body? Who or what was present?
2. Do you love yourself unconditionally?
3. Who or what do you feel gives you love unconditionally?
4. Have you ever loved someone or something unconditionally?
5. What was your family life, growing up? Did you feel loved unconditionally?
6. Are you currently, or have you been in the past, in a romantic relationship which is/was based in unconditional love?
7. Do you have a spiritual practice or religious practice which helps you feel connected to Source energy?

With your insights from these questions, find the connection which evokes a feeling of unconditional love the most for you, from the list below.

- Self-love
- Spirit love (meditation, religious)
- Partner/Romantic Love
- Family
- Animals
- Vegetation/trees

If you resonate with more than one, that is fantastic. We encourage you to read the description to all connection in which you resonate.

Self Love

If you are able to evoke unconditional love within yourself, for yourself, then your amplifying and evoking connection is gratitude. By taking yourself into a state of gratitude, you welcome the energetic vibration of unconditional love to flow through you. We recommend you develop a daily practice of gratitude. This could be a gratitude journal; contacting someone and expressing your gratitude for them; expressing gratitude to yourself; or thanking the Universe for the beauty around you. Pops of gratitude throughout your day will ensure you continuously experience unconditional love and therefore stay in a receiving state for guidance.

Spirit Love

When we speak of "Spirit Love", we are referring to the love you feel when connected to Spirit or Source Energy. Tuning into Spirit is tuning into unconditional love energy because that is what Spirit is! You may do this through meditation, or through prayer, or through creative forms of various kinds, or through simply "being." However, it is you connect to Spirit, if you are able to experience unconditional love this way, your amplifying and evoking connection is peacefulness. Daily, find moments of peace. Even one second of peace can usher in the vibration of unconditional love and allow you to receive guidance.

Romantic Love

If you have experienced unconditional love in a romantic love situation, either giving, receiving or both, then your amplifying and evoking connection is trust. Trust in all of its forms will welcome in unconditional love for you. Trust in yourself. Trust in others. Trust in the Universe. Trust in the process. Trust that everything will work out for you. Ask yourself on a daily basis, how to accept trust. Even the act of trusting yourself to make the right decision in any given moment, will welcome in unconditional love for you.

Familial Love

When we speak of family, we speak of those who create a family atmosphere for you. This may include parents, stepparents, siblings, grandparents, aunts, uncles and cousins. It may also include close friends who have stood as family for you. You define what denotes a family member for you. If you have experienced unconditional love within the family setting, your amplifying and evoking connection is unity. Unity in this context refers to the energy created within you when you act from a place of community, collective and group. It's a feeling of belonging. You are part of a team. Engaging in daily tasks which have an impact on the collective will welcome in the energy of unconditional love for you. This could be global meditations or prayer, community service, or engaging in group activities. The key is to feel the power of unity within you.

Love of Animals

If you have experienced unconditional love for or from animals, whether wild or domesticated, your amplifying and evoking connection is joy. Joy is playful and uninhibited, much like your animal friends. You may even find, the best way for you to connect to joy is by playing with or being around animals. The key to evoking joy, which in turn evokes unconditional love, is to be playful and free. Scheduling fun into your day, every day, will keep you in flow with the Universe.

Love of Vegetation and Trees

If you have experienced unconditional love while in nature or at home, surrounded by trees and plants, your amplifying and evoking connection is growth and expansiveness. You most likely are someone who loves to learn. The sense of growth which occurs when you are in the act of learning, opens you to the energy of the Universe—

unconditional love. It is the challenge of learning new things, in which you can kinaesthetically feel the expansiveness of energy. Developing a daily ritual which involves growth in a physical, emotional, mental or energetic level will evoke unconditional love within you, keeping you in flow with the Universe.

Stories of Unconditional Love
Nicole

My Love Story

LOVE HAS BEEN A DRIVING FORCE FOR ME, SINCE I WAS A LITTLE girl. If you asked me when I was young, what a successful life would look like, I would have described it in terms of healthy relationships, a loving marriage and a happy family life. Yes, I wanted career success. But the true measure of success, for me, has always been the reciprocation of unconditional love in a romantic partnership and the creation of family from it. I had few role models of this type of relationship. My parents split when I was born. My maternal grandparents were also divorced. Yet, despite everything, I had an unwavering belief in unconditional love in romance. In my heart and soul, I knew it was possible for me. I knew it wasn't just the stuff of fairy tales and Disney movies. And I searched it out!

As a teen and young woman, I developed a pattern of jumping from relationship to relationship. I loved deeply (and often, possessively). I know now that was a recipe for disaster. I dated some really wonderful guys (and some who hadn't quite found a way to express their wonderfulness!), and I pushed them away. At the time I thought

I was loving them, but what I was actually doing was smothering them. At age twenty-three, I had a significant breakup. As I healed from the breakup, I decided it was time to take a break from the continuous roller coaster of serial dating and take a long hard look at myself and my patterns in dating. I needed to be honest with myself and do whatever healing was needed, because, at the end of the day, I was the common denominator in these failed relationships. Clearly, I was attracting these dynamics and playing out a repetitive role. I made a promise to myself that I wouldn't jump into another relationship and I would give myself the gift of time, healing and honesty.

Part of my healing was tying up unfinished business I had with some of my ex-boyfriends. I had connections that had not truly finished nor transformed into friendships. One such connection was left open seven years and had me on a plane overseas to come clean and express my love and gratitude. He was in a relationship, and I had no intention of disrupting that. I needed to speak words left unsaid and let him know how significant of an impact he had had on my life. Up until that point, he was my experience in unconditional love. I loved him so much, that I truly was happy that he had found love in a relationship with another person. Honestly, I surprised myself by this realization. In the closing of romantic love, and opening of simply love of another human, I became clear in the knowing that I was ready to not only give love unconditionally but also receive it.

Have you ever had moments in your life when you felt like everything has come into alignment? Moments of clarity about the trajectory of your life? A moment in time when it all became clear how you were being prepared for this particular moment? That moment for me was when I met my husband. A friend brought him to a dinner party I was hosting. When I opened the door to welcome them in, I recognized his soul and he recognized mine. At that moment, we had no idea what capacity our connection would hold. We just knew that we were meant to be in each other's lives. Now, more than twenty years later, we know without a doubt, that we met when we had both cleared and healed enough to allow for unconditional love to flow freely and easily between us. The rest of our transformational journey has happened, and continues to happen, together. We offer each other the safe space to evolve our consciousness individually and love each other without expectations and conditions. It hasn't been all unicorns and rainbows. We have faced some significant challenges and frustrations over the years. For us, the return to unconditional love is the balm for our souls when life gets rough. When one of us is stuck in a thought pattern or energetic well, the other will say in a stern voice and a big smile, "Let me love you, damn it!" This always interrupts the patterns, as we inevitably fall into a fit of laughter.

Being in a relationship firmly rooted in unconditional love has allowed me to experience freedom. I am no longer weighed down by worry, fear, shame or guilt. Without these heavy emotions, I have also experienced a stronger connection to my intuition. I trust myself. I trust Source has my back. I trust that, if I remain in an unconditional love state, I will be shown the path forward to my goals, dreams and intentions. Ultimately, resonating in unconditional love is the most natural aspect of my being. Working with the Tri Luminii has brought me to this conscious awareness. I am so grateful for this shift as it has brought a more balanced relationship with my emotions and reactions.

Kate's Love Story with the Earth

In my early years of teaching intuitive development, I had the pleasure of sitting in circle with a woman who could best be described as the human embodiment of Mother Earth. When I was in Kate's presence, I would feel a serene strength vibe enveloping her aura. Her voice was melodic and when she would speak of her journeys into the forest, I would feel a wave of love exude from her. She loved the forest. It was her sacred space where she felt connected to all living beings and felt an overwhelming sense of expansiveness. There were no limits in energy for Kate, when she was deep within the forest. Listening to her stories could make anyone fall in love with the forest, as well!

In one particular circle I led the members through a guided meditation which entailed visiting a forest. Visiting a forest in meditation isn't unusual, but in this meditation, the focus was specifically on the plants and trees, not the animals. While everyone was gathering their metaphoric messages, Kate began to trance channel the plants and trees. We all learned a great deal about these spirits, their needs and wants, and the medicines they offer to humans and animals. It was fascinating and was the first time I had experienced a trance channeling of vegetation.

This experience sparked a new relationship for Kate. She found herself talking with the plants and trees on her daily walks in the forest. She expressed how urgent she felt in becoming a guardian for the plant life. This led to her studying botany and ultimately become a herbalist. Now, she leads people on tours of the forests, teaching about foraging, plant medicine and conservation. On her tours she trance channels the plants and trees, offering her guests an opportunity to ask the vegetation questions.

Through an unconditional love connection beginning with a simple meditation, she found her calling. She is one of many being called to be the bridge between humans and vegetation, as we embark on the journey to rejoining the ecosystem.

Michael's Journey to Self

I was working in the clinic one day when I heard a faint tap at the door. When I opened it, a young man with a sheepish grin was standing there. He apologized profusely for interrupting me (even though I repeatedly said he wasn't!) and quietly asked if he could talk with me about the intuitive circles I was hosting at the clinic. I invited him in. We hit it off immediately. Michael told me his story of struggle to follow his intuition when confronted with opposition from the strong personalities in his life. Deep within his soul, he knew what was right for him, but when these personalities believed otherwise, he second guessed himself. This act of second guessing brought up deep emotions of shame and guilt for him. These emotions were inevitably followed by anger directed at himself and at others. It was a loop he felt stuck in and wanted so desperately to be free from. He wondered if joining our intuitive circle would be the answer. At his first circle he received the guidance to start a gratitude discipline. Although he was wary of the idea, he began to write a gratitude list daily.

I didn't give much thought to the guidance after that particular circle. It wasn't until a year later that it came up again in discussion. I had noticed that Michael had started walking into the room looking more confident and sure of himself. In one particular circle he mentioned that he felt a deep sense of love and gratitude for his journey and ultimately for himself. One of the other circle members asked him how he had gotten to this place of self-love. His answer was gratitude. He had been writing his gratitude list every day since his first circle. Michael felt a shift after six months of this practice. He said he felt a growing love for himself and an opening of his intuition around the same time.

Gratitude brought him to self-love. Self-love opened his intuitive connection.

Main Takeaways from Unconditional Love

1. Unconditional Love is the energy from which we all come and to which we will all return when we complete our physical existence.
2. Unconditional Love is the vibration which unlocks and accesses Universal wisdom. It is the current of communication between realms.

3. Your connection to unconditional love is your way of preparing to receive intuitive guidance.

4. Your specific experience with unconditional love helps you identify the emotion or state of being which will raise your vibration to unconditional love.

Part One
Intuition

What is Intuition?

THERE ARE A MULTITUDE OF DEFINITIONS FOR INTUITION. FOR our purposes, we will refer to intuition as the connection and dialogue between you and Universal wisdom. This connection looks and feels different for everyone. It is important you understand this because, comparison and "should be like this", will carry you further away from the Source wisdom energy with which you are attempting to connect. Our goal in writing this book is to help you experience your own unique way of connecting to intuition. Your own *Intuitive Language.*

We encourage you to consider your intuition as one of your being's systems, like the cardiovascular system or the digestive system. In fact, it works similar to the nervous system. The nervous system sends and receives messages between the brain and the rest of the body. The intuitive system sends and receives messages between your human incarnation Self and your True Self (also referred to as the Higher Self). Your True Self is the part of you which never ceases to exist. It is fully connected to Source energy and "All That There Is". And so, when we talk of receiving guidance from Source or Spirit, it is your True Self which helps to decipher these messages. It directs the energy, then your mind provides the filter to interpret the energy.

Let us begin with how to connect to your intuition and different forms of intuitive connection.

Why Intuition is Relevant Today

From where we exist and experience you, we are aware of the immense benefits in humans developing and enhancing your intuitive connection with Spirit. In fact, it is quite puzzling why humans, in their evolution and expansion, left intuition behind. At one point in your history, your species was in tune and fully using intuition to find food, shelter, mates, etc., just like all other living beings in your ecosystem. Although this is often referred to as instincts, instincts are just the manifestation of the intuitive process. Better said, acting on one's instincts is the resulting action of following intuitive messages. It is not a long, drawn out process. It happens within a split second of receiving the intuitive hit. You can see this clearly while observing the animals and plants around you. Both animals and plants know when a storm is approaching, long before the wind picks up or the clouds roll in.

Where it is a different experience for humans, is in the understanding of intuitive messages. For thousands of years, humans have needed to know and understand everything in order to accept it as real. This development of the cognitive process was the beginning of the journey away from intuition. This was not the only factor to play in the movement away from intuition. At one time, your healers, medicine people, and wise elders, knew the importance of following intuition and working with the spirit realm. There was a harmony maintained in communities. This was also a time of humans existing as part of the ecosystem. You cared for the vegetation and they offered you their nourishment and medicine. You only hunted and used what you needed, just as the animals do. This maintained balance, which is what your planet's operating system is based upon. At all times, the individual species, along with the community of species in which it lives, is working towards balance, knowing that it is a forever dance and not a static place in which one resides. In the human body it is referred to as homeostasis. In the community in which the human resides, the human breathing waste of carbon dioxide is fed to the trees, which then feed oxygen back to the humans. Balance. Symbiotic relationships. This is where you are being called to return. And the first step to making this a smooth transition is in developing and reawakening your intuition.

It is not that you are being called to release all progress in cognitive and technological ways of being. It is that you are being called to find a way to exist with these advancements while returning to being a member of the ecosystem. The era of dominating your planet is ending. We are aware of the fear this brings to many. What will this look like? Will you be safe? Will you be able to enjoy luxuries in life? So many questions! We offer you this: You cannot even begin to imagine how wonderful the human experience will be once the need to dominate, control, steal, overpower, segregate, alienate and diminish another is removed from the collective operating system. The idea of Heaven on Earth and Utopia is not a new one. But what we speak of is beyond the conceptualization you have of this ideal. First step, first. Awaken your intuition.

Now you are being called forward to awaken the system which has been dormant in so many for millennia. Yes, you have had your sages, prophets, seers and wise people, over the generations. But these people were either deemed evil or raised to a high standard of worship-worthiness, depending on the narrative of those in power. This has sent two powerful messages to young humans as they matured and became adults, and to adults eager for a deeper connection to Spirit. Either it is dangerous to be an intuitive, or it is not real, because you couldn't possibly be as special or gifted as the "great ones." Either way, the lesson learned, was to turn off that system and listen to the wisdom of others in power, even when one feels like the wisdom being offered is not quite right. The second guessing of one's internal wisdom begins.

Before we continue with why right now, at this moment in human history, it is vital to develop your intuition, we would like to clarify what our messages and viewpoints are around a few common topics in your spiritual communities. This is not to say that our viewpoint is the only correct viewpoint. If you were to stand in front of a building and your friend was to stand at the back of the building, you would both be seeing the same building. However, your viewpoint of the details of the building and the activities happening around and within it, would be different from your friend's viewpoint. And you would both be correct. So, please understand, we are not invalidating any other channels, belief systems or spiritual concepts. We can only offer what we experience to be true, from where we exist. Although, we just offered a three-dimensional metaphor for what is actually multi-dimensional, we believe you understand the concept we are relaying.

We stand for unconditional love. It is the sole purpose of our communication through Nicole to you. Unconditional love is the energy from which you have come and the energy to which you will return, once you are complete with this incarnation. Unconditional love is what flows through every living being in the entire Universe. We offer it to you. In that offering, it would be out of alignment to speak of intergalactic wars and dark forces. We are aware there are many channels available to you, if this is what you desire to focus on. This is not our focus, nor will it ever be. From where we exist, this is not a reality. Again, it may be for others, but for us, it is not. Our message is one of unity, not divisiveness. The essence of unity is unconditional love. The vehicle to get to unconditional love in a sustainable and efficient way, is intuition.

There is no time, and yet the communication is offered to you with a focus on time. It is because, this is how you will best receive and process the information we are gifting. There is never a "most special time in human history." Every epoch has its own special focus and role to play in the continuing evolution and expansion of life on your planet. Although you may be feeling as though you are in a transition time, you are actually deep into an epoch of spiritual awakening. Humanity is ready for a different relationship with Spirit. You are being drawn to the need for connection to unconditional love. Human consciousness moves in a problem-solution focus way. The collective consciousness of your True Self's guide you to the next awakening on your journey. This guidance translates into the forming of a problem, which then leads to the need to find a solution. This satisfies the curiosity and problem-solving aspect of the human egoic experience.

The awakening you are experiencing is a result of the problem created to highlight disconnection. Slowly, your societies have been moving away from interconnectedness within community. This has created a more conscious desire for connection and compassion. Technology has been removing the energetic exchange of touch. With lockdowns across the planet, this need for unconditional love connection is heightened. The good news is the supply of unconditional love from Spirit is infinite. Opening your intuition (your channels) is the easiest and most effective way to allow the receiving of this energy. As you begin to allow yourself to receive this unconditional love, you will begin to notice your reliance on others for energy, acceptance, love and whatever else fuels you, will begin to diminish. This is when a true connection with other beings begins to open up to you. And once you experience this new way (or we should say original way) of relating, you will never want to go back to trying to manipulate, take from, or control another being, human or otherwise.

You will never hear us speak in a way which divides or segregates any beings on your planet. That would be counter-productive to our message of unconditional love! We are, however, practical in our approach and are aware that the road to being multilingual in intuitive languages, requires some boundaries and labels. In no way is one intuitive language more esteemed than another. Each and every person is able to identify with at least one intuitive language for themselves in this present moment. And each and every person has the ability to become fluent in all intuitive languages.

Communication: Medium, Guides, Angels, Higher Self, Collectives

Just as there are many forms of meditation, there are many forms of Spirit communication. These forms can be seen as a ripple in your aura. We caution you from viewing these rings as a hierarchy. You have the ability to communicate with any and all ripples in your aura. Depending on the guidance you seek, you can choose the most appropriate form of energy for the type of guidance. The closer the ring in the aura is to you, the more detailed the guidance. The farther away the ring is to you, the guidance will be in the form of more visionary or thematic-based information. We wish to express the movement of these rings is not limited to one direction. It is in all directions. Up, down, forward, backward, side to side, and a combination of all directions. It also moves in all directions in the concept of time. You can access wisdom and guidance from your past incarnations as well as your future experiences and incarnations. The sea of all there is, is accessible to each and every living energy. It is the skill of knowing when and where to dip into the sea - the skill of grasping the guidance from the ideal drop. You wouldn't ask a four-year-old child to give you guidance on solving a complex mathematical equation. Neither would you ask an elder in your community, who has never been online, for help with setting up your website. Just as you ask the appropriate person for help in the challenge you face, you can ask the appropriate aspect of the collective energy for the guidance you seek.

The closest ring is the Higher Self or True Self. In essence, this is the aspect of you which never dies, the you which travels from incarnation to incarnation. It is you without the Ego. Accessing guidance from the True Self is best suited for guidance regarding your personal journey, healing, goals, purpose and gifts you wish to share. An example would be tuning into guidance regarding a health issue you face. In this example, you can receive guidance surrounding the meaning of the challenge and how to heal. This is the practical realm of guidance—the guidance for the everyday experience. The farthest ring is "all that there is." It is the culmination of all energies, experiences, wisdom and being. It goes by many names. God. Source. Great Mystery. One. Universe. Whatever name resonates with you, use that. There is no correct name because it is all names and no name at the same time. If you need an imagery in order to connect to this energy, use something that is so vast, you can't see the end or beginning of it. We like the image of being in the middle of the ocean. As you look in each direction, it continues for what seems to be eternity. Accessing guidance from the vastness of all there is, is best suited to guidance regarding your relationship to the collective consciousness. Examples would be the themes of human evolution, global changes, and connection to other life forms on different planets. Basically, if it's a universal theme, this is the source of your guidance. That leaves all of the realms in between these rings. We are purposely not defining where they reside in relation to you because they're not truly physically in different spaces and we do not wish to create a hierarchy in your mind. Rather, we encourage you to ponder from where you would want to gather your guidance. In observing the language of your spiritual talk, we have witnessed humans getting stuck in a rut with regards to who or what they choose to contact. The labels you place upon yourselves and the energies you communicate with, are limiting your experience. In short, you are making the human experience more difficult than it needs to be. When an intuitive describes themselves as only a medium, for example, they are making a choice to only accept guidance from the aspect of energies which represent the human experience of loved ones who have transitioned. This limits their possibilities of guidance for visions and bigger picture challenges. Alternately, intuitives who "only" speak to collective energies like us are limiting their access to guidance from day-to-day challenges and goals. This is why we routinely encourage Nicole to exercise her connection to her True Self, guides, and Source energy.

We encourage you to do the same. We also encourage you to let go of the need for communication to be with a specific kind of energy. There is no problem in referring to energies by a name, to help you decipher the aspect you are communicating with. For example, speaking with guides, angels, ascended masters, fairies, elementals, and the list goes on. Use these terms as a focal point, not as a prestige point. There is no hierarchy.

Metaphors in Life

All aspects of your life offer you metaphors, consistently and constantly. Your body signals messages of what is happening in your energetic field. The sore shoulders are a metaphor for the weight of responsibility you are carrying. The knee pain is a metaphor for the resistance in moving forward with a dream or goal. The digestive issues are a metaphor for the difficulty you are experiencing in digesting an experience, thought or belief. The more chronic a physical condition is, the more unraveling there is to do in the patterns of your life. And they can all be taken care of by listening and taking action to rectify the energetic issue. There is no need for a long, drawn out process in shifting.

Your surroundings offer metaphoric and direct messages as well. On any given day you will experience multiple messages via license plates, billboard signs, overheard conversations, songs on the radio, physical sensations and random thoughts, to name a few. The key to deciphering this stimulus as to whether or not they are messages, takes practice. With clear intentions and awareness, you will begin to feel a rhythm to the way you perceive and accept messages.

The animals around you also offer metaphoric messages. Let's say on your daily walks you take note of the repeated sightings of a specific species of animal or bird. We will use the example of a squirrel. Your analytical or practical mind could easily dismiss these sightings as being a natural element of the surroundings. It may say, "yes, there are many squirrels in this area, of course I am seeing them."

While this is true, it is not the entire truth. Once you open your awareness, you will notice that some days you see more squirrels than other days. Some days, you see more squirrels of a certain colour or size, than other days. Some days, the squirrels are crossing your path and other days they are to the side of your path. Some days, you see them above you, moving about the trees, and other days they are on the ground. With an open awareness, you receive the nuances of the messages. Now, what if you are on this walk with another person, who is also aware. Does that mean you are both receiving the same message? The answer may be yes, but most likely it is no. Here is why. Firstly, you may each have a different meaning you have associated with the squirrel. For instance, for you squirrel may offer a message of quick action. For your friend, squirrel may represent resourcefulness. Secondly, you may or may not notice the same squirrels. Even if you do, the meaning attached to the way you perceive them may differ. Colours carry different meanings. Perceptions of placement (above, to the left, to the right, running backwards) will potentially have different meanings as well. So, how does the Universe orchestrate two separate messages delivered at the same time? This is part of the ornate and complex tapestry of living in flow. And the beauty is, you and your friend are also messages for the squirrels, other animals and humans you cross paths with, on your walk!

Ways to Connect

Meditation

The most common practice for connection is meditation. How do you know which form of meditation is best for you? Quite simply, try as many as you can! Each form of meditation offers something different. The more flexible you are in your ways of connecting, the easier it will be to become fluent in multiple intuitive languages. (We'll speak more about that shortly). The main goal of meditation is to clear your mind. What does that mean exactly? At any given time, you are consumed by multiple open loops (aka your to do lists and your worry lists). Meditation offers you a respite from these loops. And in this respite, you allow the words, images, feelings and knowings of Universal Wisdom to be experienced.

Meditation can be formal, like sitting and focusing on the flame of a candle or chanting a mantra. It can be active, like walking a labyrinth or walking in nature. It can be creative, like doodling or daydreaming. It can be expressive, like dancing or singing.

We like the idea of creating a habit AND having creativity in what meditation looks and feels like on a daily basis. We encourage you to stretch yourself and experience something new each day. You can take any variable and modify it. Experience meditation indoors, and outdoors. Play with the amount of time you dedicate to being in meditation. Enjoy different temperatures – meditate by a fire, or in a cold shower. Once you dedicate yourself to experiencing meditation in a multitude of forms with a multitude of variations, your mind will be opened to seeing, hearing, and feeling all of the aspects of life on your planet. This not only makes your life fuller in its expression, but also awakens your ability to receive messages in an intuitive way. You see; Spirit is in communication with you constantly. It is up to you to access this communication. The easiest way to access it, is by awakening all of your senses.

Trance

The concept of trance is generally associated with hypnosis and mindfulness activities, but there are also everyday activities in which you can partake to create a trance state. Athletes and performers refer to being in trance as "being in the zone." Ecstatic dance creates a trance state, as one is enveloped in the rhythm of the music. Any action, whether physical or mental, which brings you into a trance state will connect you to your intuition.

Trance is useful in connecting to your intuition in that it helps you focus your attention on your intentions. Your thoughts and focus define your world. When you are solely focused on an intention or an experience, it becomes your entire world.

Take a moment to pause and reflect on a time when you felt this state. It was impossible to focus on any other worldly stimuli as you focused on your desired experience at that time. In other words, your intentional focus became your world for that specific amount time in trance. Essentially, you were creating your world, as you are constantly doing. However, just like performing any project, if you focus on one or two tasks at a time versus on many tasks at once, your project will complete in a more efficient way, and much sooner.

When you are in a trance state, focused on the desired experience, you experience that experience much more quickly than if you were distracted by the plethora of stimuli of the external world. You are literally creating your worldly experience at any point in time. You get to decide if that creation is chaotic and unfocused or is aligned and in flow with your desires.

Trance Channeling

Trance channeling is different from trance. Although, it does begin with the trance we described above. Trance channeling is how Nicole channels our energies. It is the process of allowing the energies one is in communication with, to occupy the body space and speak (or type!) without the channel needing to decipher and translate the message.

*Note from Nicole about trance channeling the Tri Luminii: Trance channeling is not something I recommend to begin your channeling journey. It took me many years of practiced intuitive communication before attempting to trance channel. There are three different energies I have tranced in my lifetime, including the Tri Luminii. For me, it's a lot like dating. There is a wooing period, when we need to get to know each other's energies before we dive into trancing. I need to feel comfortable with the energies before I will allow them to occupy my physical being. This can mean having conversations for months, or years, before we attempt to trance. This is not just for my comfort. They also need to evaluate my energy and have a level of familiarity before experiencing a human experience. Once we begin trancing, it can take quite a while for the energies to acclimatize to being in physical form. They need to understand the physical sensations and physical movements, as well as access the library of vocabulary within the mind. One of my favourite memories with the Tri Luminii was when I was on vacation in Cuba with my husband. The Tri Luminii had been observing us having fun jumping waves and floating in the ocean and wanted in on the action!

They asked if they could try trancing in the water. Admittedly, I was a little nervous. They obviously didn't know how to swim, and I had visions of trying to get back into my body before drowning! Elliott, my husband, offered to spot me/us as we floated. It was a fun experience for him as well. He related back to me afterwards that it was much like the first time he helped our sons float as babies. The Tri Luminii were giddy with excitement and awe of the sensations of the water, the current and the little fish which swam up to us. They were like young children having a new experience. Once we were back on shore, the Tri Luminii expressed that the sensation of floating in salt water was similar to the floating experience in the ether (minus the sensation of wetness and little fish nipping at your feet). So, if you have ever wondered what it's like to be in spirit form, apparently, it's similar to floating in the ocean!

On a daily basis, when I begin the process of trance channeling, I first ground myself and allow myself to receive healing, cleansing and clearing from the Universe. At that point, when I feel the energetic vessel is cleansed and ready, I connect with the energies of the Tri Luminii. Perhaps you have heard people describe receiving energy as white Light entering through the top of the head and travelling down the body. I feel the Tri Luminii enter my body via the top of my head. As their energies move through my body, my egoic self and spirit step to the side of my aura. I'm still attached to my body, but I am in an observer role rather than experiencer role. It's much like watching a play from the sidelines. I can see what is happening in the background and still hear the messages they are sharing. My favourite part of trance channeling is when I experience the Tri Luminii shuffling through my vocabulary, like it's a playlist, looking for the word that is a vibrational match to message they are attempting to convey. Their search for "just the right word" is hilarious as they toss away words one after another until the perfect one is found. And then, when that word is found, there is a collective sigh of satisfaction. Immediately, that word will become a part of their own vocabulary which they will come back to easily, time and again.

Dreams (Night and Day)

Dream state. What we enjoy about communicating through dream state is the opportunity to saturate your mind with metaphors. While the critical, or logical, part of your mind is sleeping and not trying to understand or make sense of the experience, we are able to fill your mind with absurd visuals and sensations. In fact, the more absurd the better, because you are more likely to remember a dream filled with outrageous adventure than a typical everyday experience.

Being completely honest with you, we have witnessed the fascination with dream analysis with some puzzlement. It seems to be a well-loved activity amongst humans to delve into the understanding of the absurdity of dreams. For us, in Spirit and energy form, we wish to relay that these metaphors are also found in your everyday life. It may not come in an absurd form (or it might!), but it is present, nonetheless. Through the use of symbolism and metaphors, the message comes across easily. The difference between experiencing the metaphors in a dream state as opposed to everyday life, is that the outrageousness of the dream catches your attention.

We will dive deeper into discussing the symbols, metaphors and associations you experience daily as intuitive messages in later chapters. For now, understand that your waking life experience is really not that different from your sleeping life experience.

Astral Travel

Astral travel seems like a foreign concept to most people. It seems like something you would take a long time studying to master. It seems like something you need to know how to do properly. It seems like something you need to be safe about, as if it is something dangerous. It seems impossible to experience to the average person.

It is none of these things.

Not only is it none of these things; it is something every human does on a nightly basis. The difference between someone who knows they astral travel versus someone who thinks they can't astral travel is awareness. It is the act of being aware of your travelling that gives you the experience.

What did you think your spirit does while you sleep? Sit there and watch you? No! It's the time when you are free! Without the limitations of the body, your spirit can explore, witness and learn. The only thing it can't do is have a physical experience using the senses. That is, unless your conscious mind takes the journey with your spirit. It is the conscious mind which relates to the world via the senses, and therefore, translates the spiritual experience into a physical experience.

This is essentially what astral travel is - the conscious mind hitching a ride with your spirit self as it travels without the body.

Main Takeaways from Intuition

1. All sentient beings are intuitive.
2. There are a multitude of ways to connect and receive intuitive guidance. There is no one way to be intuitive.
3. Intuition is a system of the human experience, much like the cardiovascular and nervous system.

Part Two
Clairs and Clair Families

The Clairs of Intuition

When you saw the title of this book, did you think about the "clairs" (clairvoyancy, clairaudiency, clairsentience)? While identifying the clairs you play with the most is important, it is not your actual intuitive language. They do have an integral part to play in the building of your intuitive language, however. They represent the way you receive messages. One of the steps in building your Intuitive Language is identifying your clair family. Your clair family is your mode of receiving. In everyday life, you are able to determine what makes up your surroundings by using more than one of your senses. This also applies to how you determine messages from Spirit as they arrive for you. Think of the clairs as the senses of intuition. In order to experience a more robust message, you must be aware of your clair family and how it helps you to recognize signs as they appear. The clair family is comprised of your primary and secondary clairs, with some qualifying and identifying factors. We will explain it in greater detail, but first you must determine your relationship to the clairs in order to identify your primary and secondary clairs.

Discovering Your Clair

All living beings have intuitive abilities. The animals, trees, vegetation and humans are innately intuitive. The humans seem to be the ones who struggle with their connection. There are many reasons why you may be struggling with your connection. Perhaps you second guess or analyze the messages as you receive them. Or maybe you believe synchronicities are merely random coincidences. The top reason why humans struggle with their connection, though, is the belief that an intuitive message needs to be experienced in a certain way and this "way" is not the "way" you are currently experiencing guidance. Intuitive abilities look and feel different for everyone, so be patient if you are new to this. There is no hierarchy to the clairs and no "right way" to start your intuitive journey. This exercise is a fun way to discover your strongest "clair" - the clair that is already present within you.

For this exercise you will need a piece of paper, pen and a comfortable place, where you won't be disturbed or distracted. Give yourself the plenty of time for this exercise. Allow yourself to be fully immersed in the process. Most importantly, enjoy it!

Using the entire page (single spaced and normal-size writing!), describe the best vacation of your life. Before you begin writing, close your eyes, take some deep breaths and imagine yourself on this vacation. Use all of your senses to be present to the experience. Then, open your eyes and begin writing in as much detail as possible. Don't stop until the page if full!

Now, take out five different coloured pencil crayons or highlighters - yellow, orange, green, blue and red. Circle or highlight all of the words which can be considered "seeing" words, yellow. For example, colours, shapes, objects. Circle or highlight all of the words which can be considered "hearing" words, blue. For example, sounds of the wind, foliage, birds, people and animals. Circle or highlight all of the words which can be considered "feeling or physical," orange. For example, smells, tastes, temperatures, textures and sensations you experienced. Circle or highlight all of the words which can be considered "emotional or feelings," green. For example, actual emotions or feelings about things in your experience and using the words "I feel." Circle or highlight all of the words which can be considered "thinking" words, red. For example, thoughts that reminded you of something, thinking about certain things, using the words "I think" or "I know."

Now hold the page in front of you. Which colour stands out the most? And notice if there is a big difference between the number of words for each colour. Maybe there is one predominant colour, or maybe it's a fairly evenly split between two, or perhaps more. Here is what it means for you:

- Mostly yellow = you are primarily clairvoyant
- Mostly blue = you are primarily clairaudient
- Mostly orange = you are primarily clairsomatic
- Mostly green = you are primarily clairemotive
- Mostly red - you are primarily claircognitive

Clairvoyant

When you receive messages in a visual manner you are being clairvoyant. A clairvoyant is aware of objects, shapes, and colours, as messages being conveyed throughout their day. In meditation, a clairvoyant will "see" images with their mind's eye. When most humans consider channeling, they usually think of clairvoyancy. Yet, this is only one of the five ways in which you can communicate with Spirit.

Clairaudient

When you receive messages in an auditory manner you are being clairaudient. A clairaudient is aware of sounds, voices, and songs, as messages being conveyed throughout their day. In meditation, a clairaudient will "hear" messages. This can be words spoken by Spirit, a song which plays in your mind, or other sounds.

Clairsomatic

When you receive messages as physical sensations, you are being clairsomatic. A clairsomatic uses their body as a barometer for tuning into energy vibrations. Clairsomatics tend to be the strongest energy healers and energy shifters.

Clairemotive

When you receive messages as emotions or feelings, you are being clairemotive. A clairemotive processes the energy of messages through emotions and feelings. Clairemotives are strongest with their gut instincts and can feel when something is right or wrong for them.

Claircognitive

When you receive messages as a knowing or thought, you are being claircognitive. A claircognitive experiences thoughts or "knowings" as they receive the vibration of energy from Spirit. The challenge for the claircognitive is in deciphering a message versus an egoic thought. There is a great discipline in quieting your mind in order to receive the claircognitive message.

Clairsentient

Clairsomation, clairemotion, and claircognition are often grouped together under the category of clairsentience. Clairsentience refers to the experience of receiving messages through feelings, whether they be physical, emotional or mental. When identifying your clair family, you will use the umbrella category of clairsentience, with the identifying features of the either clairsomation, clairemotion or claircognition, if your primary or secondary clairs are one of these.

Now that you are clear on which clairs are your strongest, you can begin the process of identifying your clair family. The clair family is the mode in which you receive guidance and is the final step in building your intuitive language before we bring it all together.

Your Primary Clair

IN THE PREVIOUS EXERCISE YOU DISCOVERED YOUR PRIMARY clair. We encourage you to play with this and become comfortable with using your primary clair on a daily basis. We have a fun activity for you to strengthen your relationship with your primary clair.

For this exercise you will want to keep a notepad handy throughout your day. At the beginning of your day, decide you would like to gain more insight on a specific topic. Perhaps you are contemplating a career shift, or want to find a life partner, or you are making a decision about a move. At the top of a fresh page in your notebook, write the topic you are looking for which you desire more guidance. Go about your day as you normally would. Perform your regular tasks. The exercise is one for becoming aware of the communication you receive through your primary clair. It is important to continue with your daily activities, because you will soon become aware that you are receiving intuitive guidance constantly, even in the most mundane circumstances.

If your primary clair is clairaudience, make note of everything you hear. Songs on the radio; overheard conversations; and especially how many yes's and no's you hear. At the end of the day, notice what repeated or was a theme. How can this relate to your chosen topic for guidance?

If your primary clair is clairvoyance, make note of everything that catches your eye. Words on billboards; license plates; colours; animals; etc. By the end of the day, you will experience a theme or be able to decipher a clear yes or no to your question.

If your primary clair is clairsomation, clairemotion, or claircognition, you will fall within the clairsentience category. Be sure to monitor your sensations, thoughts and feelings throughout the day. What scents are you aware of? What emotions show up for you? Do you perceive different tastes, randomly? Are there common textures you experience throughout the day? Do you experience different temperatures when thinking certain thoughts? Someone who has clairsentience as their main clair is guided by their feelings and physical experiences. If this is you, your answer will be more about how the question or theme makes you feel rather than a specific action-oriented guidance.

At the end of the day, take a look at the information you have gathered intuitively. What trends or patterns do you see? Can you decipher a concrete message from your findings with regards to your specific question or topic? When you wake the next morning, complete this exercise again. Perhaps you need some clarity from the messages you received the day before. Or perhaps you want to continue with the same theme. What is important is that you repeatedly perform this exercise. Each time you will notice the nuances of how Spirit communicates with you. You will begin to create a personalized dictionary of words, objects, sounds, emotions, thoughts and sensations. Just like learning any new language, the more you immerse yourself in it, the quicker you become fluent in communication with Spirit.

Once you feel a rhythm in the receiving of guidance, you can expand and test this ability. There is a game which Nicole plays with her Flow members each month. It is called the Power of Three. The idea is to receive confirmation that you have ready the signs correctly with regards to the question you have asked of Spirit. It was first designed with the clairvoyant-dominant in mind and so, the original instructions went as follows:

- If you have an idea of an action you would like to take to move your goals forward but are not confident that it's the best course of action, then ask for three identical signs to be shown to you within a twenty-four-hour period. You want to choose something possible but not necessarily probable. For example, ask to see three orange cars to confirm that you are on the right track.
- If you have no idea what to do next, ask for the message to come to you in three clear ways within the next twenty-four hours. Then remain open and aware. For myself, I usually receive these messages in the form of songs on the radio, billboard signs, vanity plates or partially overheard conversations.

Here is how to modify this process if your primary clair is not clairvoyance:

- If your primary clair is clairaudience, instead of three cars, ask for three songs with a specific word in their title. Make it a word that is possible but not probable.
- If your primary clair is clairsentience, decide which of the aspects of clairsentience you resonate with the most. Feelings, thoughts, textures, scents, tastes or temperatures? Let us use the example of scents. You would ask for confirmation of your interpretation of your guidance by asking to smell, three times, a specific scent which is possible but not probable.

We recommend you change the signs each time you play the Power of Three. Once you are feeling comfortable with receiving guidance via your primary clair, and confirming it with the Power of Three, you are ready to move onto the next step in developing your intuitive language. Developing your secondary clair.

Your Secondary Clair

IF THE PRIMARY CLAIR REPRESENTS THE FOUNDATION OF A building, then the secondary clair represents the frame. When you build the frame on the foundation, it begins to look like a house. Once you attach the secondary clair to your primary clair, you will begin to see a structure to your intuitive language. This is where your unique communication skills start to develop. Getting comfortable with the primary clair is the biggest step on your journey to freely communicating with Spirit. We promise you that it only gets easier from here!

Your secondary clair adds finesse to your communication style. It gives a deeper and more robust message. To identify your secondary clair, return to the test you completed earlier. The colour which was second most commonly highlighted is your secondary clair.

We're not going to make this complicated for you! The exercises you took part in to strengthen your primary clair are the same ones you will do with your secondary clair. There is one extra layer though. You will verify your messages and/or confirmations via the Power of Three game AND your primary clair. Here is a recap of the exercises:

1. At the beginning of your day, decide on a specific topic you would like to gain more insight on. We suggest choosing something new, or at the very least a new aspect of the topic you used in these exercises for the primary clair.

2. At the top of a fresh page in your notebook, write the topic you are looking for guidance on. Go about your day as you normally would. Perform your regular tasks. The exercise is one for becoming aware of the communication you receive through your secondary clair. It is important to continue with your daily activities, because you will soon become aware that you are receiving intuitive guidance constantly, even in the most mundane circumstances.

3. If your secondary clair is clairaudience, make note of everything you hear. Songs on the radio; overheard conversations; and especially how many yes's and no's you hear. At the end of the day, notice what repeated or was a theme. How can this relate to your chosen topic for guidance?

4. If your secondary clair is clairvoyance, make note of everything that catches your eye. Words on billboards; licence plates; colours; animals; etc. By the end of the day you will experience a theme or be able to decipher a clear yes or no to your question.

5. If your secondary clair is clairsentience, monitor your sensations and feelings throughout the day. What scents are you aware of? What emotions show up for you? Do you perceive different tastes, randomly? Are there common textures you experience throughout the day? Do you experience different temperatures when thinking certain thoughts? Someone who has clairsentience as their main clair is guided by their feelings and physical experiences. If this is you, your answer will be more

about how the question or theme makes you feel rather than a specific action-oriented guidance.

6. Without focusing specifically on your primary clair, make note of any signs which arrive via your primary. This will take some practice, as you've just spent a period of time focused on your primary clair!

7. At the end of the day, take a look at the information you have gathered intuitively. What trends or patterns do you see? Can you decipher a concrete message from your findings with regards to your specific question or topic?

To verify your understanding of the messages, play the Power of Three game using your secondary clair.

1. If your secondary clair is clairvoyance, ask to be shown three identical items as confirmation.

2. If your secondary clair is clairaudience, ask for three songs with a specific word in their title. Make it a word that is possible but not probable.

3. If your secondary clair is clairsentience, decide which of the aspects of clairsentience you resonate with the most. Feelings, thoughts, textures, scents, tastes or temperatures? Using the example of feelings or emotions, you would ask for confirmation of your interpretation of your guidance by asking to spontaneously feel high levels of joy (or whatever emotion you would like to insert here). Remember, it must be possible but not probable. Therefore, if you know you will be visiting an amusement park, you will choose the feeling of excitement or exhilaration, you could choose a feeling such as peacefulness or gratitude.

When you wake the next morning, complete this exercise again. Perhaps you need some clarity from the messages you received the day before. Or perhaps you want to continue with the same theme. What is important is that you repeatedly perform this exercise. Each time you will notice the nuances of how Spirit communicates with you. You will begin to create a personalized dictionary of words, objects, sounds, emotions, thoughts and sensations. Just like learning any new language, the more you immerse yourself in it, the quicker you become fluent in communication with Spirit.

Once you are feeling comfortable with receiving guidance via your secondary clair and confirming it with the Power of Three and your primary clair, you are ready to move onto the next step in developing your intuitive language. Identifying your clair family.

Clair Family

When Spirit speaks with you, it is in the form of story. More specifically it is metaphorical story telling. Storytelling, as you experience it, can be experienced in many different forms. When speaking of the clair families, there are certain types of storytelling which are more in alignment with the communication style of each family. We've related them to specific life experiences with which you may be familiar. When we describe each experience, take a moment to imagine you are in the story experience and access the type of listening that would be required of you, to "get" the story. There are three story experiences. We have the film experience, the campfire experience and the book experience. Before continuing with this chapter and diving into each clair family, take a moment to think about each of these story experiences. Which one do you resonate with most? Which one is a challenge to conjure up? Now, it's time to identify the story of your clair family!

The clair family is made up of your primary and secondary clair. The combination of the two clairs create a specific type of communication style with Spirit. The only exception to this rule is when your primary and secondary clairs fall within the clairsentience category.

If this is your experience, you will build your clair family in the following way. Your primary clair is clairsentience and your secondary is the more frequent presence of clairvoyance or clairaudience, in the exercise you completed in discovering your clair. Another note we wish to make is in the distinction of the clair families involving clairsentience. Each of the sub-categories of clairsentience give a descriptor of the family. If your primary and secondary clairs are within the clairsentience category, please read the description of both sub-sections for the family. For example, if your primary is clairsomatic, your secondary is clairemotive and your tertiary is clairaudience, you would look to the descriptions of the Expressive Conversationalist and the Emotive Conversationalist.

Listed below are the clair families. Each family is a combination of two clairs. Find the family which is comprised of your primary and secondary clair. Then read, through the rest of the family descriptions. You may find yourself in a little of some or even all clair families. There are similarities between the families and catching these nuances will only help to serve you in becoming fluent in multiple intuitive languages. But we'll get to that later!

The Observer
(clairaudience • clairvoyance)

IF YOUR PRIMARY AND SECONDARY CLAIRS ARE CLAIRAUDIENCE and clairvoyance, you are a member of the Observer clair family. The Observers, once trained in their intuitive language are genius at picking up on the metaphors in their surroundings. They are able to combine the seeing and the hearing in order to observe the message they are constantly receiving from Spirit.

The Observer's story telling experience is best related to watching a movie. The film experience is filled with sounds and visuals. The Observer absorbs the story line and all of its nuances through the sights and sounds. They have a deep understanding of the hidden messages in the movies, as well. The movie experience is a personal one. Although you may watch a movie with another person, the experience is not dependent on another human (other than the actors in the movie). For this reason, the Observer develops their intuition on their own time and without reliance on others. This is not meant to say that they would not benefit from being in group. They would use the group to deepen their experience by finding their messages in other people's messages.

The movie-watching skills translate well into the Observer's communication with the Universe. With practice, the Observer becomes aware of the metaphors presenting themselves as random forms in nature, billboards, songs, license plates, logos and tag lines.

An area of expansion for the Observer is in bringing their awareness inwards. With practice, they become nimble at catching messages outside of themselves. The challenge is in internalizing stimuli. There is a sense of safety in keeping energy outside of themselves. By welcoming in the unconditional love of the Universe, they expand their awareness and grow into a more well-rounded and responsive receiver. If you are an Observer, we suggest starting with developing your claircognitive abilities. This will seem less foreign to you than clairsomatic and clairemotive.

The Conversationalist
(clairaudience • clairsentience)

If your primary and secondary clairs are clairaudience and clairsentience, you are a member of the Conversationalist clair family. The Conversationalists feel and listen their way through communication with the Universe. They are aware of their changing sensations in the body and can feel the congruence of sounds and words which are synchronistic with their messages.

The Conversationalist's story telling paradigm is best relayed as a campfire experience. Imagine a group of friends gathered around a fire, sharing stories. There is the physical sensation of the heat from the fire and the coolness of the air. There is the energy generated by the bodies present. The smells of the wood burning. The sounds of the crackling fire. The tastes of the marshmallows or hot dogs cooked over the flame. The sensations generated by the campfire experience only serve to enhance the story telling. There is a complete feeling for the Conversationalist. They feel connected and satiated by the full sensory experience.

As we mentioned, the clairsentience is the umbrella clair for clairemotion, clairsomation, and claircognition. Each of these specific clairs offer a more directed sensation within conversation.

The clairaudient-clairemotive is the Emotive Conversationalist. Using the analogy of the campfire stories, the clairemotive connects with the scary ghost stories told by the campfire. They are energized by the spike in emotions in storytelling. When communicating with Spirit, their messages will be heightened by paying attention to the emotions which are evoked as they listen to the conversations around them and within them. Songs on the radio can stir up emotions which can then translate into messages of next steps to your path to manifestation.

The clairaudient-clairsomatic is the Expressive Conversationalist. Using the campfire stories, the clairsomatic connects with the stories which are acted out. A clairsomatic resonates with movement and expression through the body. When communicating with Spirit, their messages will be heightened by the feelings and sensations they feel within their body. Coupled with the clairaudience, a clairsomatic will notice how certain sounds, songs, words, and vibrations feel within them. It is through this communication, they are able to translate the vibrations into messages.

The clairaudient-claircognitive is the Wise Conversationalist. Within the campfire setting, this would be most in alignment with stories which have a lesson imbedded in them. The claircognitive mixed with clairaudience is able to tap into their "knowing" when prompted by sounds, words, and vibrations.

An area of expansion for the Conversationalist is within their own clair family. This begins with the clairsentience aspect of the Conversationalist family. Your primary and/or secondary clairs are within the clairsentience, so the best place to begin your expansion is within the clairs of the clairsentience category. You are someone who is in tune with your internal environment. Further expansion is in developing the ability to focus outwards.

Some questions to ponder:

- Do you hold fear in seeing the outside world?
- What is it that you don't want to see?

- What would happen if you let the world into your inner space?

As you can sense from these questions, opening your intuition is also a journey of self-discovery. As you navigate the opening of clairvoyance you will begin to relate to the world around you in new and exciting ways. The messages received visually will resonate with you, physically, giving you a deeper understanding of the guidance you are receiving.

The Explorer
(clairvoyance ✦ clairsentience)

IF YOUR PRIMARY AND SECONDARY CLAIRS ARE CLAIRVOYANCE and clairsentience, you are a member of the Explorer clair family. The Explorers feel and see their way through communication with the Universe. They are aware of their changing sensations in the body and can notice these changes as they see visuals.

The Explorer's storytelling paradigm is best relayed as a book experience. Imagine a great novel, where you get lost in the story completely. When an Explorer reads a novel, they are able to see themselves in the scenarios of the characters. They are able to feel into the bodily sensations the characters are experiencing. They become the characters as they read the story. They become an explorer of the book's world—imagining the sites and sensations along the way.

Within the umbrella of the clairsentient aspect of the Explorer, we can focus more specifically on each of the clairsentient subsections.

The clairvoyant-clairemotive is the Romantic Explorer. Keeping with the paradigm of stories through books, the most aligned book experience would be the romance novel. The Romantic Explorer can see themselves in the scenarios as well as feel the emotions, which are always plentiful in romance novels! Every visual description is filled with emotional connections. This is how the Romantic Explorer receives messages and guidance from Spirit. They are stimulated by the visual experiences which then evoke an emotion. The message is found in the combination of emotion and picture.

The clairvoyant-clairsomatic is the Adventurous Explorer. Their book experience would be an action/adventure story. The Adventurous Explorer can see themselves in the adventures and feel the adrenaline rushes of the characters and scenarios. They have a visceral response to visual stimuli. As the Adventurous Explorer receives messages, one of two experiences will happen. In the first scenario, they will receive a visual message, such as a billboard sign or come across an animal while hiking. When this is meant to be part of a message from Spirit, it will be accompanied by a sensation in the body. The second scenario is flipped. First the physical sensation is felt, then it is followed by a visual message. The difference here is that the visual message is usually within their mind. For example, if they feel stiff in the knees and then have a mental image of their vision board, this could be interpreted as a resistance to moving forward with their goals. The knees represent movement forward. The vision board represents their goals. As the Adventurous Explorer hones their intuitive skill, they will begin to notice what certain sensations mean for them, especially as they are received in conjunction with a visual sign.

The clairvoyant-claircongnizant is the Intellectual Explorer. Their book experience is the travel or cultural book. For the Intellectual Explorer, there is a mixture of sight and thoughts. A book filled with pictures from other lands and cultures would be stimulating for them. It would encourage dreaming and creating a vision of possibilities. The Intellectual Explorer will often have ideas and visuals just "come to them," without explanation. The challenge lies in the deciphering of what is their own imagination and what is a message from Spirit. This comes with practice and paying attention to the outside world as much as the inside world. The Intellectual Explorer tends to be quite introverted and is quite comfortable to remain in their own inner world. Finding the balance and the joy of connection in the outer world is an achievement worth celebrating. Once the Intellectual Explorer can do this, they will find their communication with Spirit is fluid and done with great ease.

An area of expansion for the Explorer is, similar to the Conversationalist, in developing the clairs of clairsentience. Once you feel comfortable in fully experiencing the clairs of clairsentience, your next stretch is in developing clairaudience. As an Explorer, you dance between the outside world and your inner world. Clairaudience offers a place of balance for the two extremes. What is it that you have not wanted to hear? Or what have you heard in the past that disturbed you? These are questions to ponder if you find yourself in a state of resistance to opening your clairaudience.

Main Takeaways from Clairs and Clair Families

1. The clairs are not the Intuitive Languages.
2. There are five main clairs: clairvoyance, clairaudience, clairsomation, clairemotion, and claircognition.
3. Clairsentience is the umbrella term for clairsomation, clairemotion and claircognition.
4. Your primary and secondary clair form your clair family.
5. There are three clair families:

Observer (clairvoyance + clairaudience)
Conversationalist (clairsentience + clairaudience)
Explorer (clairsentience + clairvoyance)

Part Three
Intuitive Languages

What are Intuitive Languages?

WHAT ARE INTUITIVE LANGUAGES? WHY WOULD YOU WANT TO
know yours? When do you use your intuitive language? How can
being aware of your intuitive language help you in your everyday life?

Just like communication between humans looks, sounds and feels
different; communication between humans and Spirit also looks,
sounds, and feels different depending on the human who is communicating. And while we will focus on the main intuitive languages, we
remind you that everyone has their own unique expression within
these languages. Why would anyone want to know what their intuitive language is, let alone learn a new one? The answer is simple.
Any change, healing, transformation, manifestation, situation, object,
relationship, feeling, habit, or experience you desire is easily attain-
able when you are in dialogue with Spirit. It also applies to your
everyday life experiences. We have heard some people express
concern around the perceived lack of personal responsibility when
one relies on guidance from Spirit for life experiences and creations.

Here is our answer to this concern. At all times, you as the
human, are having the life experience. You are the one living with the
consequences of manifestation. You are the one deciding you want

something different. You are the one creating your reality. Spirit is your team member. Your answer from Spirit will always be yes. The guidance to the finish line is like having a pilot hover over your race, advising you of the clearest path to the finish line. It is always your choice to take, or not to take, the advice. It is always your choice how fast or slow you proceed. And should you choose not to take the advice, you will never be abandoned by Spirit, nor run out of options. Possibilities are infinite. Please read that again. Possibilities are infinite. Wouldn't it be wonderful to be able to access that guidance? Imagine having this lifeline available to you 24/7. Wouldn't it be a relief to know, you don't need to do it all on your own? This is why it is important to know and understand your intuitive language. You are already receiving this guidance on a daily basis. You just may not be catching it because it's like someone is speaking to you in a foreign language. Let's get this cleared up for you now. So, that starting today, you can begin actively communicating with Spirit and accessing this celestial support system.

Creating the Environment to Receive

The first step to building your intuitive language, is defining how you best prepare to receive. This is necessary, because not everyone receives in the same way. Creating a space around yourself and within yourself, which is conducive to your energy and your way of being, will set you up for a clear receiving of messages. We have witnessed so many people interested in being in communication in Spirit, playing a passive game. Can you imagine being in conversation with someone, and you are doing all the talking? It wouldn't be much of a conversation, would it? When you begin to perceive the receiving of messages as a conversation, not a lecture, you contribute to the flow of energy. It is in the flow of energy, where you receive. Without it, there is no receiving. Please understand, this is not about testing you. Quite the opposite - it is about co-creating an experience together. The more you make it playful, the more you will get out of it. Think about your fondest memories. They are about fun times with other humans, or animals, or in nature.

In order to determine your ideal space for receiving in the easiest way, we're going to look into the different types of environment in which you connect with best. If you love to travel or enjoy a variety of settings, this element of your intuitive language may be the most difficult to nail down. We offer to you that, if this is your experience, you are actually in a good position for being fluid in an element of your receiving from Spirit. Still, we encourage you to hone in on one element which applies most of the time. It doesn't mean you will be missing out on the other elements. We promise!

Here are some questions to ask yourself, to focus in on your ideal environment. Please answer them with the best answer. In other words, the answer that applies most of the time:

1. In what setting do you feel most alive? Rural or Urban?
2. Where do you feel most connected to Spirit? Rural or Urban?
3. In what setting do you feel most free? Rural or Urban?
4. In which setting are you best able to focus? Rural or Urban?
5. In which setting are you most aware of your surroundings? Rural or Urban?
6. Where do you feel in awe, most often? Rural or Urban?
7. In which setting do you think most clearly? Rural or Urban?

Notice which setting you chose the most often - rural or urban. If you chose rural, you are most aligned with nature in its natural setting. If you chose urban, you are most aligned with community and therefore thrive in a social setting. The nuances of these environments expand as we dig deeper into each one.

Urban Environment

If you are most aligned with urban environments, you are more likely to become aware of guidance when you are either in commune with others or surrounded by others. You thrive intuitively when you are in proximity to other humans. The buzz of energy generated by other humans is invigorating for you. You are a social being, whether it is expressed in an introverted or extroverted way.

Developing your space externally and internally to receive messages form Spirit, involves creating a sacred space amongst others. In an optimal situation, you would find yourself in a social space like a community park, cafe, or cultural centre. If it is not possible to be in these spaces, creating a similar space indoors is ideally. You could surround yourself with pictures of friends and family. You could play ambient noises, re-creating the atmosphere of being in a busy cafe. Whatever helps you feel connected to others, will prepare you for receiving messages from Spirit.

Rural Environment

If you are most aligned with rural or natural environments, you are more likely to become aware of guidance when you are alone and outdoors. You thrive intuitively when you are in proximity to the natural world. Animals, plants, trees, rocks and waters provide a calming and connected presence for you. Whether you enjoy the company of others or not, you feel most in tune with Spirit when you are alone. It is for this reason that traditional concepts of meditation are more likely to be in alignment with you.

Developing your space externally and internally to receive messages from Spirit, involves creating a sacred space just for you. In an optimal situation, you would find yourself outside, alone in a natural setting, free from the noise of others and man-made objects such as vehicles. When preparing to receive, you want to ensure you will not be disturbed. If you can't be outside, then bring the outdoors indoors. This could include creating a sacred space with plants, crystals, water, fire (candles or incense). If there are specific animals you align with, have pictures or statues of these specific beings. The important aspect of creating a space is that you feel connected to the natural world, while also being able to reflect inwards.

Ideally, find a space outside in which you resonate. Nicole has a favourite spot in her town's main parkland. It is by a river and is filled with lots of trees and various wildlife. This is a go-to place for her when she needs to reconnect or recharge. Your place could be a beach, a forest, a desert, a lake or any other natural space.

Now let's take this creation of environment, this preparation to receive, to a metaphoric level. As we dive deeper into the building of your Intuitive Language, you will soon come to realize how the world of intuition is best experienced through metaphor. This is largely due to the fact that, as children, you were programmed with morals and life lessons through fairy tales and cultural stories. They were metaphors and they were received beautifully by your developing mind. Spirit loves to make communication with you easy. This is why we speak through metaphor mostly, at least until you can sit in conversation with Spirit, as you would with a friend at your local coffee shop. You will get there—with practice!

If you resonated with the rural environment, you will find a list of natural elements, below. Rate them, from 1 to 7 (one being the most attractive), in order of personal attraction or affinity. Some of these scenarios overlap. For instance, you may enjoy visiting a park that has a forest, open play area and a river within it. Then you would ask yourself, is it the forest or the open parkland or the river which you feel most attracted to? We understand that it may depend on the day. But for the most part, you will find that you are more attracted to one more than the others. So, using this example, you may find that when you visit this park, you spend most of your time wandering in the forest, then sit by the river, and are less likely to be in the open park space. Then you would rate forest (1), water (2), and parkland (3).

- Beach (ocean or lake)
- Desert (sand or tundra)
- Flowers, plants, but not trees
- Forest, trees
- Parkland
- Water (rivers, lakes, waterfalls, ocean but not on the beach)
- Mountains, rocks - structure

Remember we are using these elements and scenarios as metaphors, to help you prepare to receive your intuitive guidance. Yes, you can literally go to a beach to meditate, but maybe you don't live by a beach. You're not going to hop onto a plane each day in order to receive guidance! Instead, you can create this environment or energy for yourself on a daily basis. Here are the metaphoric meanings of the elements you were most drawn to:

Beach (ocean or lake)

If you were drawn to the idea of being on a beach, you are more easily able to access intuitive guidance in a dreamy state. What this means, is you are most open when the environment allows you to be dreaming. This can be a daydream-like state, or it can be through your dreams at night. Setting up your surroundings to encourage dreaminess is your first step in building your intuitive language.

Desert (sand or tundra)

If you were drawn to the idea of being in a desert, whether that is a hot, sandy desert, or a cold arctic tundra, you are more easily able to access intuitive guidance in a space that is simple, clutter-less, expansive and free from distraction. You would not be one who would do well with meditating in a small, enclosed space. You need the feeling of expansion in order to receive guidance.

Flowers and Plants (but not trees)

If you were drawn to the idea of being around flowers and plants, you are more easily able to access intuitive guidance when you are surrounded by beauty. In fact, you are probably someone who is able to see the beauty in most things. Consider setting up your surroundings with your favourite colours and textures. Perhaps having inspirational images could evoke an opening awareness for you.

Forests and Trees

If you were drawn to the idea of being in a forest or around trees, you are more easily able to access intuitive guidance once you have rooted or grounded yourself. A simple exercise of coming into your body fully and connecting with the Earth, is a great way to begin your day or to reset yourself during the day.

Parkland

If you were drawn to the idea of being in a parkland, you are more easily able to access intuitive guidance when you are in a playful atmosphere. When there is a sense of freedom and joy, you are most open. What can you do each day to create a playful atmosphere for yourself?

Water (rivers, lakes, oceans, but not on the beach)

If you were drawn to the idea of being in or around water, but not on the beach as that's another option, then you are more easily able to access intuitive guidance when you are flowing with your day and not limited by too much structure. This is not to be confused with distractive living! You enjoy variety in your day, and this is a necessary component to being open to communication with Spirit. For you, there is power in being able to sustain a certain level of dancing with your day. It is in that power and joy which you receive intuitive guidance openly.

Mountains and Rocks

If you were drawn to the idea of being in the mountains, or around rocks, you are more easily able to access intuitive guidance when you have structure. This can come in the form of scheduling your day, or having a set place where you connect, or even having a go-to method for connecting or meditating. Routine is your friend. It gives a sense of safety and security. In that place of structure, you are able to take in vast amounts of information and guidance.

If you resonated with the urban environment, you will find a list of urban scenarios, below. Rate them, from 1 to 7 (one being the most attractive), in order of personal attraction or affinity. Some of these scenarios overlap. For instance, you may enjoy attending a sporting event at a community park. Then you would ask yourself, is it the sporting event or the community park which you feel most attracted to? We understand that it may depend on the day. But for the most part, you will find that you are more attracted to one more than the others. So, using this example, you may find that when you attend these sporting events at the local community park, you enjoy spending most of your time chatting with others in the community more than watching the actual game. Then you would rate community park (1), and sporting events (2).

- Cafe
- Community park
- Cultural centre (art gallery, museum, etc.)
- Walking through neighbourhoods
- Busy city streets
- Shopping malls
- Sporting events

Remember we are using these elements and scenarios as metaphors, to help you prepare to receive your intuitive guidance. Yes, you can literally go to an art gallery and receive messages. But you're not going to visit an art gallery every day in order to receive guidance! Instead, you can create this environment or energy for yourself on a daily basis. Here are the metaphoric meanings of the scenarios you were most drawn to:

Café

If you were drawn to the idea of being in a café, you are more easily able to access intuitive guidance when you are in a cozy atmosphere. What feels cozy to you? What can you add into your spaces on a daily basis to create this cozy atmosphere? We encourage you to use all of your senses to create this atmosphere for yourself.

Community Park

If you were drawn to the idea of being in a parkland, you are more easily able to access intuitive guidance when you are in a playful atmosphere. When there is a sense of freedom and joy, you are most open. What can you do each day to create a playful atmosphere for yourself?

Cultural Centre

If you were drawn to the idea of being at a cultural centre, like an art gallery or museum, you are more easily able to access intuitive guidance when you are in an inspired space. How can you begin your day in an inspirational way? What can you surround yourself with, in your personal space, which will continuously inspire you?

Walking Through Neighbourhoods

If you were drawn to the idea of walking through neighbourhoods, you are more easily able to access intuitive guidance when you are in connection with one or a few others. You thrive on intimate connection. Starting your day connecting with a close friend or loved one is ideal. Make time throughout your day for interactions with others to keep the flow of messages coming your way.

Busy City Streets

If you were drawn to the idea of walking through busy city streets, you are more easily able to access intuitive guidance when you are either in movement yourself or surrounded by movement. What others would consider to be distractions, help you to focus inwards easily. If you are not able to get out and move around, consider having moving water like a water fountain in your workspace. Fidget toys can also be useful to you.

Shopping Malls

If you were drawn to the idea of being in a shopping mall, you are more easily able to access intuitive guidance when you have variety and choices available to you. You thrive in changing environments. How can you inject something new into each day? It can be as simple as taking a different route to work.

Sporting Events

If you were drawn to the idea of being at a sporting event, you are more easily able to access intuitive guidance when you are in a team or collective environment. Being in a yoga or meditation class would work well for you. Surrounding yourself with reminders of groups you belong to, is an easy way to evoke this atmosphere for you.

Stories About Environment
Nicole

A Lesson from Sue

THE VAST MAJORITY OF GUIDED MEDITATIONS, INCLUDING THE ones I have guided with my students, are situated in natural settings. In a guided meditation you will generally find yourself on a beach, in a forest or on a mountain. I think this is because nature naturally grounds and recharges us. However, a student of mine let me know this is not the ideal place to feel connected, safe and peaceful for everyone!

Sue was having difficulty connecting in our meditations. I noticed as everyone else had peaceful, serene facial expressions during the meditations, Sue was antsy and looked uncomfortable. I thought maybe she was just having difficulty finding a comfortable position, but when we talked after one of the sessions, I found out it was the meditations that were making her feel uncomfortable.

She told me that she always hated being in nature. She hated the idea of being near wildlife and bugs. The darkness of a night sky in the wilderness scared her immensely. The quiet was disturbing. And the feeling of being alone, to fend for herself, was what she took along with her into these types of meditations, even though she knew she was really just sitting in her chair, safe in circle with us.

So, I asked her what sort of places she feels connected to Spirit. When does she feel alive? Her answer was the complete opposite to the setup I had created in our meditations. She felt connected in urban settings. The energy and buzz of the city makes her feel like she is connected to all living things (even those bugs and wildlife in the forest!). Her dream vacation is touring the cities of far-off lands, being with the people, and experiencing the tastes and smells of these places.

This opened my mind. And as the Tri Luminii dictated the words for the urban connection, I immediately thought of Sue. It's important to remember that there are many ways to feel connected. In fact, you might be a combination of the two. On further contemplation, I realized that I am. I'm not one for huge crowds or bustling city streets. I do, however, feel the connection while sitting in a cafe (in fact parts of this book have been written inside one!), exploring art galleries, or walking through neighbourhoods and parks.

Keep in mind, connecting with other humans, is also connecting with nature, because we are a part of the ecosystem of this beautiful planet.

Ivan's Winter Wonderland

This is not a meditation, or even an intuitive story. I was working with a hypnosis client years ago, guiding him to create a safe place within his mind in which he could imagine himself when he felt overwhelmed or triggered.

In this type of session, I ask specific questions to conjure up imagery and evoke the power of the unconscious mind to create the perfect scenario for the individual. This session took a turn that surprised the client and inspired a big change in his life.

As we started to dive into the creation of a safe place, he started to describe an expansive space. This was not an uncommon place for people to start. It often led to being in a field or even a desert. His next description came out almost as a question. He said, "it's all white and I feel cold". Then he started to laugh and said that is mom used to joke with him as a child that he should've been born in the arctic, the way he preferred a cold room to sleep in and hated the summer months. He had created a safe place in the arctic tundra. I asked him to describe the safe feeling he felt when in the tundra. Ivan's face lit up as he talked about the expansiveness of the vista and the simplicity of everything being white. He felt like it was a blank canvas to create whatever reality he desired. This felt profound on so many levels and gave me a lot to work with in our session. Years later our paths crossed, and I told him that his safe place creation left a lasting impression with me. He was excited to report that a year after our session he signed up for an arctic adventure in the Yukon. He relayed stories of seeing the Northern Lights and snowshoeing across the tundra. While on this vacation, he connected with an indigenous community and immediately felt like he had come home. This connection inspired him to raise awareness of issues the indigenous communities of the North face on a daily basis. His initiatives have him traveling frequently to the Yukon, which suits him just fine!

Building your Intuitive Language

THERE ARE FIVE STEPS IN BUILDING YOUR INTUITIVE LANGUAGE. Building your intuitive language is like preparing for a journey. First, you ensure you have a suitcase. In the Intuitive Languages, this would be the environment—the way you prepare to receive. Then you ensure you have the essentials - the toiletries and undergarments. This is your connection to unconditional love and is the state of being in which you receive. Next, you have the basic clothes you match everything with. This is your primary clair—your easiest mode of receiving guidance from Spirit. Now you're ready to think of the shoes and specialty clothes, jewellery and accessories which make the outfits unique. In Intuitive Languages, this is your secondary clair— your second easiest mode of receiving guidance. Finally, we have the items that make your journey extra special—the items you use to enhance your experience like books, cameras, and journals. This is identifying your clair family.

We are sure most humans reading this will want to jump right to the clair family and stay there, but we implore you to follow the path of the map we are laying before you. While we are sure you received a great deal of insight when you discovered your clair family, bringing each of the steps together will feel more complete. By beginning with the environment, you are ensuring your foundation is strong. Then, moving into your relationship with love, and setting up your state or way of being, you will feel grounded and certain in your ability to receive messages. As you add your clair family, you will quickly begin to become aware of the messages you are constantly receiving from Spirit. Although this process is about building your intuitive language, we know this will also be a wonderful journey of self-reflection and will help you to understand your communications with others and yourself. It is our intention that you are able to identify how you play you in your Earthly experience.

Are you ready to build your language?

Bringing it All Together—Your Intuitive Language

Now it is time to bring it all together! The formula for determining your Intuitive Language is simple.

Environment + Unconditional Love + Clair Family
= Intuitive Language

The first component is your relationship to environment. This is the way you prepare your surroundings in order to receive. In the chapter on Environment, you examined your relationship to your surroundings; where you felt safe and connected to all beings. There were two over-arching categories. You were either connected to the urban environment or the rural environment. Within each of those categories, you learned about your unique connection style. For the purpose of determining your Intuitive Language, we will remain in the over-arching categories. The urban environment is translated to "social" in the Intuitive Language. The rural environment is translated to "natural."

The second component to your Intuitive Language is your relationship to unconditional love. This is the way you prepare your inner being for receiving. In other words, this is the state of being you reside in as you prepare to receive. In the chapter on Unconditional Love, you learned about how best connect to unconditional love and what the corresponding amplifying emotion is to help you into this optimal state. There are six different emotional connections: self-love; spirit love; partner or romantic love; familial love; animal love; and vegetation love. For the purpose of formulating your Intuitive Language, these will be grouped into two categories. If your connection to love was best felt in self-love or spirit love, then the second element to your Intuitive Language is Ethereal. If your connection to love was best felt in partner/romantic love, animal love, familial love, or vegetation and tree love, then the second element to your Intuitive Language is Grounded.

The third, and final component to your Intuitive Language is your clair family. It is simply the name of your clair family.

To recap: your Intuitive Language is formulated by adding your relationship to the environment plus your relationship to unconditional love plus your clair family. Let us offer you a couple of examples.

Example A

1. You determined the environment in which you feel most connected and alive is the urban environment. Your first component in your Intuitive Language is Social

2. You determined your relationship to unconditional love was felt the strongest in your romantic partnership. Your second component in your Intuitive Language is Grounded.

3. You determined your clair family to be the Observer. Your third component in your Intuitive Language is Observer.

4. Putting it all together now, your Intuitive Language is Social Grounded Observer (SGO).

Example B

1. You determined the environment in which you feel most connected and alive is the rural environment. Your first component in your Intuitive Language is Natural.
2. You determined your relationship to unconditional love was felt the strongest when you are meditating as so, you align with Spirit love. Your second component is Ethereal.
3. You determined your clair family to be the Explorer. Your third component in your Intuitive Language is Explorer.
4. Putting it all together now, your Intuitive Language is Natural Ethereal Explorer (NEE).

Now you're ready to learn about your Intuitive Language. Below you will find the details about each of the Intuitive Languages.

Social Ethereal Observer (SEO)

The Social Ethereal Observer (SEO) is someone who is energized by the sounds and sights of being around other humans. They thrive in community. Seeing and hearing the energy generated by others brings them into alignment.

A Social Ethereal Observer (SEO) will receive intuitive messages best when they are out in society or connecting with at least one other person. Paying specific attention to the physical signs such as billboards, road signs or slogans on the clothing others are wearing, as well as overhearing aspects of conversations or songs on the radio. Before venturing out to connect with others, setting an intention for guidance on a specific topic will help decipher what visuals and sounds are messages.

Although a Social Ethereal Observer (SEO) thrives in community, they experience a challenge in identifying messages when communing with large groups of people. This is because the Ethereal aspect of their intuitive language is more naturally focused on receiving messages when they are alone in community. This seems like a paradox. Are they social or not? They are indeed social, but they have a tendency to be givers when in community, and in doing so, they may miss out on their own messages. For this reason, we encourage a commitment to seeing oneself in others. This will ease the transition into being able to see, hear or feel the message for the self through another's experience.

A heightened attunement to intuitive messages occurs when the Social Ethereal Observer (SEO) maintains a state which allows them to feel light, dreamy and flowing with the sights and sounds surrounding them.

Social Ethereal Conversationalist (SEC)

The Social Ethereal Conversationalist (SEC) is someone who is energized by the sounds and sensations of being around other humans. They thrive in community. Allowing themselves to experience the energy vibrations generated by the sounds of others brings them into alignment. This is experienced in their specific clairsentient sub-category (clairsomatic, clairemotive, or claircognitive).

A Social Ethereal Conversationalist (SEC) will receive intuitive messages best when they are out in society or connecting with at least one other person. Paying specific attention to the sounds such as over-heared aspects of conversations or songs on the radio and how they experience these sounds in a sentient way, will lead them to their messages. Before venturing out to connect with others, setting an intention for guidance on a specific topic will help decipher what sounds and sensations are messages.

Although a Social Ethereal Conversationalist (SEC) thrives in community, they experience a challenge in identifying messages when communing with large groups of people. This is because the Ethereal aspect of their intuitive language is more naturally focused on receiving messages when they are alone in community. This seems like a paradox. Are they social or not? They are indeed social, but they have a tendency to be givers when in community, and in doing so, they may miss out on their own messages. For this reason, we encourage a commitment to seeing oneself in others. This will ease the transition into being able to see, hear or feel the message for the self through another's experience.

A heightened attunement to intuitive messages occurs when the Social Ethereal Conversationalist (SEC) maintains a state which allows them to feel light, dreamy and flowing with the sounds surrounding them and the sensations within them.

Social Ethereal Explorer (SEE)

The Social Ethereal Explorer (SEE) is someone who is energized by the sights and sensations of being around other humans. They thrive in community. Allowing themselves to experience the energy vibrations generated by the visuals around them, brings them into alignment. This is experienced in their specific clairsentient sub-category (clairsomatic, clairemotive, or claircognitive).

A Social Ethereal Explorer (SEE) will receive intuitive messages best when they are out in society or connecting with at least one other person. Paying specific attention to the visuals they encounter such as billboards, road signs or slogans on the clothing others are wearing, and how they experience these sounds in a sentient way, will lead them to their messages. Before venturing out to connect with others, setting an intention for guidance on a specific topic will help decipher what sounds and sensations are messages.

Although a Social Ethereal Explorer (SEE) thrives in community, they experience a challenge in identifying messages when communing with large groups of people. This is because the Ethereal aspect of their intuitive language is more naturally focused on receiving messages when they are alone in community. This seems like a paradox. Are they social or not? They are indeed social, but they have a tendency to be givers when in community, and in doing so, they may miss out on their own messages. For this reason, we encourage a commitment to seeing oneself in others. This will ease the transition into being able to see, hear or feel the message for the self through another's experience.

A heightened attunement to intuitive messages occurs when the Social Ethereal Explorer (SEE) maintains a state which allows them to feel light, dreamy and flowing with the sights surrounding them and the sensations within them.

Social Grounded Observer (SGO)

The Social Grounded Observer (SGO) is someone who is energized by the sounds and sights of being around other humans. They thrive in community. Seeing and hearing the energy generated by others brings them into alignment.

A Social Grounded Observer (SGO) will receive intuitive messages best when they are out in society or connecting with at least one other person. Paying specific attention to the physical signs such as billboards, road signs or slogans on the clothing others are wearing, as well as overhearing aspects of conversations or songs on the radio. Before venturing out to connect with others, setting an intention for guidance on a specific topic will help decipher what visuals and sounds are messages.

A heightened attunement to intuitive messages occurs when the Social Grounded Observer (SGO) feels grounded, sure, certain and there is a clear intention set for receiving guidance.

Social Grounded Conversationalist (SGC)

The Social Grounded Conversationalist (SGC) is someone who is energized by the sounds and sensations of being around other humans. They thrive in community. Allowing themselves to experience the energy vibrations generated by the sounds of others brings them into alignment. This is experienced in their specific clairsentient sub-category (clairsomatic, clairemotive, or claircognitive).

A Social Grounded Conversationalist (SGC) will receive intuitive messages best when they are out in society or connecting with at least one other person. Paying specific attention to the sounds such as overheard aspects of conversations or songs on the radio and how they experience these sounds in a sentient way, will lead them to their messages. Before venturing out to connect with others, setting an intention for guidance on a specific topic will help decipher what sounds and sensations are messages.

A heightened attunement to intuitive messages occurs when the Social Grounded Conversationalist (SGC) feels grounded, sure, certain and there is a clear intention set for receiving guidance.

Social Grounded Explorer (SGE)

The Social Grounded Explorer (SGE) is someone who is energized by the sights and sensations of being around other humans. They thrive in community. Allowing themselves to experience the energy vibrations generated by the visuals around them, brings them into alignment. This is experienced in their specific clairsentient sub-category (clairsomatic, clairemotive, or claircognitive).

A Social Grounded Explorer (SGE) will receive intuitive messages best when they are out in society or connecting with at least one other person. Paying specific attention to the visuals they encounter such as billboards, road signs or slogans on the clothing others are wearing, and how they experience these sounds in a sentient way, will lead them to their messages. Before venturing out to connect with others, setting an intention for guidance on a specific topic will help decipher what sounds and sensations are messages.

A heightened attunement to intuitive messages occurs when the Social Grounded Explorer (SGE) feels grounded, sure, certain and there is a clear intention set for receiving guidance.

Natural Ethereal Observer (NEO)

The Natural Ethereal Observer (NEO) is someone who is energized by the sounds and sights of being around in nature. They thrive in a natural environment when connecting with animals, vegetation, water, rocks, crystals and the elements. Seeing and hearing the energy generated by the natural world brings them into alignment.

A Natural Ethereal Observer (NEO) will receive intuitive messages best when they are in a natural setting or imagining themselves to be in one in meditation. Spirit communicates with them through animals and the natural elements. Paying specific attention to the sights and sounds which draw their attention in nature, will help them identify the messages Spirit is sending them. Before venturing out to connect in nature, setting an intention for guidance on a specific topic will help decipher what visuals and sounds are messages.

A heightened attunement to intuitive messages occurs when the Natural Ethereal Observer (NEO) maintains a state which allows them to feel light, dreamy and flowing with the the sights and sounds surrounding them.

Natural Ethereal Conversationalist (NEC)

The Natural Ethereal Conversationalist (NEC) is someone who is energized by the sounds and sensations of being around the natural world. They thrive in nature. Allowing themselves to experience the energy vibrations generated by the sounds of nature brings them into alignment. This is experienced in their specific clairsentient sub-category (clairsomatic, clairemotive, or claircognitive).

They thrive in a natural environment when connecting with animals, vegetation, water, rocks, crystals and the elements. Hearing and feeling the energy generated by the natural world brings them into alignment.

A Natural Ethereal Conversationalist (NEC) will receive intuitive messages best when they are in a natural setting or imagining themselves to be in one in meditation. Spirit communicates with them through animals and the natural elements. Paying specific attention to the sounds which draw their attention in nature and then being aware of the sentient experience resulting from these sounds, will help them identify the messages Spirit is sending them. Before venturing out to connect in nature, setting an intention for guidance on a specific topic will help decipher what sounds and sensations are messages.

A heightened attunement to intuitive messages occurs when the Natural Ethereal Conversationalist (NEC) maintains a state which allows them to feel light, dreamy and flowing with the sights and sounds surrounding them.

Natural Ethereal Explorer (NEE)

The Natural Ethereal Explorer (NEE) is someone who is energized by the sights and sensations of being around the natural world. They thrive in nature. Allowing themselves to experience the energy vibrations generated by the visuals of nature brings them into alignment. This is experienced in their specific clairsentient sub-category (clairsomatic, clairemotive, or claircognitive).

They thrive in a natural environment when connecting with animals, vegetation, water, rocks, crystals and the elements. Seeing and feeling the energy generated by the natural world brings them into alignment.

A Natural Ethereal Explorer (NEE) will receive intuitive

messages best when they are in a natural setting or imagining themselves to be in one in meditation. Spirit communicates with them
through animals and the natural elements. Paying specific attention
to the visuals which draw their attention in nature and then being
aware of the sentient experience resulting from these sights, will help
them identify the messages Spirit is sending them. Before venturing
out to connect in nature, setting an intention for guidance on a
specific topic will help decipher what sounds and sensations are
messages.

A heightened attunement to intuitive messages occurs when the
Natural Ethereal Explorer (NEE) maintains a state which allows
them to feel light, dreamy and flowing with the sights and sounds
surrounding them.

Natural Grounded Observer (NGO)

The Natural Grounded Observer (NGO) is someone who is energized by the sounds and sights of being around in nature. They thrive
in a natural environment when connecting with animals, vegetation,
water, rocks, crystals and the elements. Seeing and hearing the
energy generated by the natural world brings them into alignment.

A Natural Grounded Observer (NGO) will receive intuitive
messages best when they are in a natural setting or imagining themselves to be in one in meditation. Spirit communicates with them
through animals and the natural elements. Paying specific attention
to the sights and sounds which draw their attention in nature, will
help them identify the messages Spirit is sending them. Before
venturing out to connect in nature, setting an intention for guidance
on a specific topic will help decipher what visuals and sounds are
messages.

A heightened attunement to intuitive messages occurs when the
Natural Grounded Observer (NGO) feels grounded, sure, certain
and there is a clear intention set for receiving guidance.

Natural Grounded Conversationalist (NGC)

The Natural Grounded Conversationalist (NGC) is someone who is energized by the sounds and sensations of being around the natural world. They thrive in nature. Allowing themselves to experience the energy vibrations generated by the sounds of nature brings them into alignment. This is experienced in their specific clairsentient sub-category (clairsomatic, clairemotive, or claircognitive).

They thrive in a natural environment when connecting with animals, vegetation, water, rocks, crystals and the elements. Hearing and feeling the energy generated by the natural world brings them into alignment.

A Natural Grounded Conversationalist (NGC) will receive intuitive messages best when they are in a natural setting or imagining themselves to be in one in meditation. Spirit communicates with them through animals and the natural elements. Paying specific attention to the sounds which draw their attention in nature and then being aware of the sentient experience resulting from these sounds, will help them identify the messages Spirit is sending them. Before venturing out to connect in nature, setting an intention for guidance on a specific topic will help decipher what sounds and sensations are messages.

A heightened attunement to intuitive messages occurs when the Natural Grounded Conversationalist (NGC) feels grounded, sure, certain and there is a clear intention set for receiving guidance.

Natural Grounded Explorer (NGE)

The Natural Grounded Explorer (NGE) is someone who is energized by the sights and sensations of being around the natural world. They thrive in nature. Allowing themselves to experience the energy vibrations generated by the visuals of nature brings them into alignment. This is experienced in their specific clairsentient sub-category (clairsomatic, clairemotive, or claircognitive).

They thrive in a natural environment when connecting with animals, vegetation, water, rocks, crystals and the elements. Seeing and feeling the energy generated by the natural world brings them into alignment.

A Natural Grounded Explorer (NGE) will receive intuitive messages best when they are in a natural setting or imagining themselves to be in one in meditation. Spirit communicates with them through animals and the natural elements. Paying specific attention to the visuals which draw their attention in nature and then being aware of the sentient experience resulting from these sights, will help them identify the messages Spirit is sending them. Before venturing out to connect in nature, setting an intention for guidance on a specific topic will help decipher what sounds and sensations are messages.

A heightened attunement to intuitive messages occurs when the Natural Grounded Explorer (NGE) feels grounded, sure, certain and there is a clear intention set for receiving guidance.

Bilingual and Multilingual

COMMUNICATION FEEDS CONNECTION. WHEN YOU TRAVEL TO A foreign land and at least attempt to speak key phrases in their local language, you develop a connection. From this place you are able to find other ways to enhance your communication—hand gestures, sounds, drawing pictures, etc. This continues to deepen your connection. In other words, you find ways to ensure you are understood. In that moment, you are open to seeing, hearing and experiencing communication in new ways.

Being in communication with Spirit works in a similar way. Spirit works with you to send you the guidance in all forms. Your job is to learn and figure out what it all means. And Spirit never stops trying to get its message across to you! It will show you the visuals. It will send you the sounds. Songs will evoke an emotional response which trigger a message or give you validation. Sensations will develop in your body. What seems like a random thought, will come to mind at just the right time to steer you on your path.

Once you feel confident communicating in your Intuitive Language, you are encouraged to begin to explore the other languages. In doing so, you create a conversation with Spirit which is not only easier to navigate, but richer in its messaging to you. When you combine your Intuitive Language, with even just one other Intuitive Language, you will have a greater perspective of the guidance being given to you. Also, by stretching yourself out of your comfort zone, you create a renewed sense of wonder and curiosity.

We suggest easing yourself into becoming bilingual. Pick an Intuitive Language which has the same relationship to environment and to unconditional love as your Intuitive Language. For example, if you are a Social Ethereal Explorer (SEE), your relationship to environment is social and your relationship to unconditional love is ethereal, so choosing to work with the language of Social Ethereal Conversationalist (SEC) would be a great start because it also has the social and ethereal connections.

Asking for validation of your interpretations via your Intuitive Language, will help you become confident in your ability to catch the messages in your bilingual attempt. When you are feeling comfortable communicating with Spirit in the two languages, continue to move on to the other Intuitive Languages which have the same relationship to environment and unconditional love as yours. Once you have exhausted these, move on to the Intuitive Language which has the same relationship to environment and clair family as yours. In other words, the one with the opposite relationship to unconditional love. Using our earlier example, of your Intuitive Language being Social Ethereal Explorer (SEE), you would move onto Social Grounded Explorer (SGE). Followed by Social Grounded Conversationalist (SGC), and so on.

Main Takeaways from Intuitive Languages

THE FORMULA FOR BUILDING AN INTUITIVE LANGUAGE IS: Relationship to Environment + Relationship to Unconditional Love + Clair Family.

1. Your connection to environment is your way of preparing your external environment to receive intuitive guidance.
2. Your relationship to environment, when forming your Intuitive Language, will either be Social (S) or Natural (N). This is the first element of your Intuitive Language.
3. Your relationship to unconditional love, when forming your Intuitive Language, will either be Ethereal (E) or Grounded (G). This is the second element of your Intuitive Language.
4. Your clair family is the third element of your Intuitive Language. This will be either Observer (O), Conversationalist (C), or Explorer (E).

Part Four
Living in Flow

A Note About Living in Flow
Nicole

WHEN I FIRST FORMALLY LEARNED MEDITATION FOR THE SOLE purpose of communication with Spirit, I was introduced to the concept of metaphors in meditation. In fact, I still teach meditation and intuitive development in this manner. In my classes, a typical guided meditation will have a few pit stops where you see, sense, feel, or just know that, an object is there. Then, when you come out of meditation you begin to translate the meaning of that object. The questions I often offer to my students are, "What does a (insert object) mean to you?" or "What makes (object) different from other (objects of a similar category)?" This begins the reflective process of defining your personalized intuitive dictionary.

This personalized intuitive dictionary can also be applied to everyday experiences. Shortly after I began learning this method of intuition, I became aware of many of the items I was seeing in meditation, showing up in real life. I'm a patterns and research nerd, so I started tracking it. What was I thinking about at the time? What intentions had I recently set? What decisions was I contemplating? I soon realized that seeing these items in real life was also a message from Spirit. To test it, I asked Spirit if I am correct in interpreting these items as messages, then please show three yellow cars today. It became a playful game. This too was a message because the more fun I had with it, the more frequent the messages arrived. Or maybe, better said, in my lighter and playful state, I was much more aware of the messages being given to me.

This is flow.

Using Your Intuitive Language to Live Life in Flow

Whether you choose to strengthen your intuitive skills into the development of other languages, or not, you have the opportunity to consciously begin living your life in flow, now. What do we mean by "flow?" Flow is the state of allowing oneself to be in the rhythm of one's own internal energies, the energies of world around them, and the Universal energies. In this state, one is able to communicate harmoniously with Source energy and the Universe at large, within a complex system of ever-flowing energy. This is flow state, as we define it. The "knowing" that you are in it, is the awareness of the constant communication. To be anywhere, at any time, and to be able to pinpoint the guidance and/or confirmation for your desired journey, is to be in flow.

This, in turn, generates a feeling of unconditional love. In this feeling of unconditional love, you also contribute to the flow messages to other living beings. There is a never-ending cycle of giving and receiving; of working symbiotically to uplift one another. As you continue along your evolutionary path as humans, this is the calling to which you are awakening. This world is not just for you. It is for you to share, experience, and thrive with other beings. These beings have been giving to you continuously for millennia. Now it is time for you to join the conversation. This begins with listening.

The listening comes in many forms and there are many levels of accessing, processing and comprehending. To begin your listening practice, we suggest you look to the first two steps of building your Intuitive Language. Your relationship to the environment and your relationship to unconditional love will guide you to the easiest place to start. We are about to give you a variety of ways to start living in flow. It is not to overwhelm you, it is to inspire you and encourage you to see how easy it is to be in flow. Take your time in implementing these ideas. They are meant to be fun and playful. The moment you feel this is work, stop. That is a sign that you are in need of digesting and assimilating the new practice. Let it be. Then, when you feel a pull to continue on, pick up where you left off. It is the fun and light energy that keeps you moving and remaining in flow.

Meditation with Purpose

As much as we encourage you to practice the art of recognizing metaphors life offers you on a daily basis, we also encourage you to develop a meditative practice. Specifically, we recommend a meditative practice with purpose. This purpose is to be in communication with Spirit—for guidance, for inspiration, for reassurance.

When you combine the focus and connection of meditation with the focus of a question or intention, you open up to a conversation. Here is an easy way to begin a meditation with purpose.

In your journal, write about something for which you would like guidance. Perhaps you have a specific question. If you don't have a specific question, write about the theme or topic on which you would like guidance. Some common themes are health, relationship issues, career or business path, and purpose. There are no limits to the questions you can ask. By writing about the topic, you begin your trance and opening to connection with Spirit. You enter into flow. Once you feel yourself connecting with the topic, and beginning to relax, close your eyes and take some deep breaths. Allow the breaths to take you into a deeper connection, a deeper relaxation. Then imagine there is a box in front of you. Lift the lid and see, sense, or feel what is inside. Then, come out of meditation and translate the image you saw inside the box. Ask yourself, "What does a (insert object) mean to me?" or "What makes (object) different from other (objects of a similar category)?" This is your guidance regarding the topic of intention you chose. To change things up, instead of opening a box you could imagine opening a door, unveiling a piece of art, or putting on headphones and listening for words or music (this is especially ideal if clairaudiency is your primary clair).

The Importance of Being in Group

When you think about times in the past in which you were learning life skills, you were most likely in a group setting. Whether that group was family, community or school, there were others there with you. Fundamentally, you are a social species. Being in community is how you have thrived for millennia. In fact, it is your natural instinct (aka intuition) to belong in community. There is a feeling of safety, connection, and purpose. When a group of people with a similar goal for learning and expansion come together, everyone's growth expands exponentially.

This is even more relevant for the development of intuition. Let us explain why. As you open and become aware of the messages you are constantly receiving, you will naturally doubt them. You will especially doubt the ones which feel good but go against logic. At the same time, you will blow off the messages that are logical, because you will think, "Well, obviously!" Spirit knows this and is cleverly one step ahead of you! Messages come in many forms, from many vehicles of communication. Just because you are aware of a message in one form, does not mean that you aren't receiving validating or expansive messages in multiple other forms. When you choose to develop your intuition alongside a group of other intuitives, Spirit will orchestrate these messages to be given within each group member's message. In other words, the messages which come through for one, come through for all.

Each month in my Flow group, the members gather together to be guided through a meditation. In this meditation there are strategic moments when the members receive a metaphoric message. After the meditation is complete, they come back together and translate their messages. While each member's message is uniquely theirs, relevant to their situation and their specific ask for guidance, there is a theme which begins to emerge. This is an overarching message, pertaining to each person present, which validates and expands the individual message they received. For those members who listen closely, they will also receive a key word or feeling in each of the individual messages. It is an art and requires practice, and it is available to everyone. The key is in finding the balance of giving, in the form of holding space and curiosity for the person translating their message, and receiving, in the form of catching the words and feelings which are also messages for you within that person's message. If you are too focused on one aspect of this equilibrium, you will not be able to receive your message. Too much focus on the person translating means you will miss your own cues.

We encourage you to find a group of intuitives with whom you resonate, to practice and evolve your intuitive skills. Your intuitive growth will be exponential in nature as a result.

Understanding Your Rhythm with Cyclical Changes

Life on Earth runs in cyclical patterns. The seasons. The days. The nights. The lunar phases. Birth, death, and rebirth. Everything has a time, a place and a pattern of both. These cycles are not just outside of you, but also within you. You are a part of the cycles and the cycles are part of you.

There is a unique rhythm to how you navigate the cycles. This rhythm is special to you. No one will be exactly the same. You will naturally find, as you continue to develop and evolve your intuitive skills, identifying patterns within the cycles you live will come easier and easier.

Here is our suggestion. Start with the big cycles. These are the ones in which you travel with others. Examples of these would be the seasons, days of the week, moon cycles, and decades of age.

We have a quick exercise to share with you, which will get you started in familiarizing yourself with cycles. Grab a pen and paper. For each season of the year, answer the following questions. If you live close to the equator and don't experience major changes in the seasons, answer the questions based on stormy season versus dry season:

1. What is your relationship to this season?
2. In what activities do you enjoy partaking?
3. What are your moods like during this season?
4. What foods do you feel drawn to during this season?
5. What are your energy levels during this season?

When you begin to better understand your natural rhythms within various cycles, you will find living in a flow state to be much easier and enjoyable.

Communing with Nature: Rejoining the Ecosystem

Once upon a time, a long, long time ago, there was a species called humans, who lived in harmony and symbiotically with all other species. And then, one day, they realized they had the mental capacity to make life better for themselves and to dominate all the other species on the planet. While this worked well for them for a few thousand years, they reached a time when they needed to rejoin the ecosystem on their planet, if they were to continue to thrive.

We do not mean to ridicule or make light of the human journey. In fact, every invention and technological advance has been a response to intentions set for development and easing the challenges of life. We do' however, wish to relay the importance of shifting away from a human-centric view of life, into one which is collaborative and honouring of all species of your beautiful planet. Now, this does not mean you unlearn all of the advances in technology and systems which humanity has invented thus far. It means finding a way to incorporate these with the natural world.

As you become stronger in using your Intuitive Language, you will become more and more aware of the messages you receive in your everyday life. One of the simplest ways for Spirit to send you a message is through the natural world. This is because nature is constantly in the flow of Universal energy. There is no resistance. And you, in turn, are the messenger of guidance to the animals and vegetation around you. It is a symbiotic relationship; working together in harmony, to uplift and nourish all living species.

Earth is a planet of balance. Physically, as humans, you naturally move towards homeostasis. For every action, there is a reaction. Every ailment has its cure. Trees receive your carbon dioxide and give you oxygen. Every time you give, you also receive. And every time you receive, you also give. This is how the flow of energies on this planet correlate. Any breakdowns or congestion of energies are simply a result of the imbalance of giving and receiving. Respecting and caring for the Earth and all of her inhabitants makes space for the Earth caring for you as well. Can you imagine how beautiful life will be on Earth when humans rejoin the ecosystem and not only live in harmony with each other but also with every living being on the planet? This doesn't need to be "just" a dream. You have many entities wishing you guide you through this process, if you will allow us.

Listening

When we speak of listening, we are not speaking of hearing. There is a difference between hearing and listening. Listening requires a focus. Listening requires attention. Attention to understand. Attention to find a solution or common ground. Listening can be an intention for learning or understanding. It is like hearing with love and compassion. When you bring yourself into an unconditional love state, you are listening. If you are in a conversation, whether with another human, animal, plant form, Spirit, or even with yourself; if you are in it to be right, if you are in it to control the conversation, you are not listening. If you are in it to be in a place to rise yourself up and not bringing those with you up as well, you are just hearing, not listening.

Let's talk a bit about how to prepare or prime yourself for listening. Let's use the example of engaging in a difficult conversation or a conversation which has the potential for being difficult. If you raise your energetic vibration, either into unconditional love energy, or something which is close to it, for example gratitude or joy, then you are ready to come into that conversation and be in a listening place. As you are listening, you will know just when to say the "right thing", or that which will be heard by the other person, in just the right way. When we say this, we don't mean in order for you to win an argument or win your idea over. That is not the intention. So, pay attention to what your intention is as you enter into this conversation. Realizing that when you bring your energy into a higher state, a higher vibration, you are resonating at a level in which pure communication happens. It will just naturally happen. It will just naturally be in the best interest of all involved; and those who will come in contact with those involved as well.

There are many ways to listen. Of course, there is sound—there is listening to the words. There is also listening to the feeling. What are you feeling from that in which you are in communication with? Use all of your senses and use your clairs. In order to decipher, as to whether or not you are in a pure listening place at any point in time, you can check in and see how you feel. Are you feeling like you are in that state of unconditional love, or the equivalent state which resonates with you, or have you dipped back down? If you have dipped back down, be gentle with yourself. Be kind and compassionate with yourself. Allow yourself to raise that vibration again to bring you back to that listening place.

We wish to share about the topic of listening for many reasons. We feel it's important at this time, because as we witness communication, we notice that listening is not the human's strong suit. This comes from many different reasons. We do not blame or shame you for this. We understand that it could be the child of trauma that is not listening, that is deep within you. It can be high impatience levels and you just want to get on with it. It can be a feeling of, "if I truly listen to this intuitive message, this guidance to move me forward, then I'm going to have to stretch myself". And that might be uncomfortable. So, it could be your resistance that's not listening. Just check in with yourself. Do it from a place of non-judgement. Do it from a place of curiosity. Do it from a place of wondering how this could be a better experience for yourself. You'll know you're in this listening place when you find yourself becoming more and more energized by the communication. You will feel a rush of energy.

Can you imagine for just a moment what it would be like if world leaders were to stop, bring their vibration up to the frequency of unconditional love and then be in communication with one another? There would be no wars. There would be so many solutions achieved. There would be so much growth and opportunity for all living beings on this planet. This isn't a pipe dream any longer. You are at a place on your planet, where this is more accessible than ever before. And the average person, as much as we are not in favour of that phrase, can tune into their vibration; can tune into the vibration of others and all around, very easily, by learning to listen, learning how to tune into their intuition, and using their Intuitive Language.

Know that as you focus on this, as you bring your energy state into the unconditional love, the ability to listen, you are automatically sending a wave of that energy across the planet. We have an exercise for you to experience this way of listening, in action.

Be near a plant or an animal. Choose whichever you are most in alignment with. Raise your vibration to an unconditional love state. Then just listen. Listen to what they have to say to you. You'll feel it. Notice how you feel it in your body. Notice how certain thoughts come to your mind. Notice how the animal or plant begins to move in reaction to your energy. If you're feeling especially daring, ask the plant or animal a question. Be curious and patient. There will be a response. It may not come in the way you are expecting, so hold your assumptions and expectations at bay. If you remain in this state, with patience, you may even experience a dialogue of sorts between you and the plant or animal. Notice how they listen to you. Is it different from your listening? What is similar? We realize you may second guess yourself and believe you are making it up. But ask yourself this, why did you think what you thought or felt what you felt?

Now, what if you apply this exercise to your communications with other humans, or even with yourself? How would this improve your life?

Synchronistic Living

Living in synchronicity. It's something you used to do, as a species, before the advent of technology and the stepping away from the natural world. Animals live synchronistically. Technically, you are an animal, therefore, you have the programming deep within your DNA. It's time to awaken it.

What is synchronistic living? Essentially, it's living in flow. There is a certain level of trust or faith required in order to jump into the river of life and let her take you on the journey. What we want to say to you about this is—at any point, you can stand up and walk out of the river. If you need a break, a pause, or a re-assessment of your intentions, simply step out of the flow. In an "all or nothing" approach to life, which so many humans subscribe to, this can feel unnatural. But we encourage you to take these pauses often. It helps you to appreciate the journey thus far and gain more clarity for your desired checkpoints along your journey of life.

Synchronistic living is a simple three-part process. The first step is to set an intention. What do you want to manifest in your life? What experience do you want to have? Who do you want to become? The second step is when your Intuitive Language comes into play. It is when you tune your awareness for the signs the Universe will send your way. These are signs of confirmation that your intention is a good one for your growth and overall life path. There are signs for tweaking your intention. For example, if you set an intention for a life partner and have listed out the specific qualities you are searching for in this partner, the Universe may have you cross paths with someone who exemplifies these qualities. In experiencing them, you may realize there is some tweaking needed for some of the qualities.

While both of these types of signs are extremely important in helping you to focus your energy, the most important are the signs which most people ignore. These are the action signs. You are co-creating your life experience with the Universe. That means you need to take action and be an active participant in the manifestation process. Each next step of your journey is being shown to you all the time. Luckily, the Universe is infinitely patient and never stops supporting you in your intentions. And so, the third step of the synchronistic living process is completely in your hands. It is to take action on the guidance.

The process is a simple one, and it also takes practice. Be compassionate with yourself and remember to step out of the river from time to time. This is not a race. You are not in competition with anyone. And you will never be abandoned by Spirit. We are with you, always.

Main Takeaways from Living in Flow

1. Flow is the state of allowing oneself to be in the rhythm of one's own internal energies, the energies of world around them, and the Universal energies.
2. It is recommended to step in and out of flow on a regular basis.
3. There is no "right" way to be in flow.

Main Takeaways from Living in Flow

1. Flow is the state of allowing oneself to be in the rhythm of one's own internal energies, the energies of world around them, and the Universal energies.
2. It is recommended to step in and out of flow on a regular basis.
3. There is no "right" way to be in flow.

Wrapping It All Up

We have shared a lot of information to process. We acknowledge this fact and encourage you to be gentle with yourself as you continue your journey with your Intuitive Language. Our intention in sharing this process with you is one of support and ease of communication with Spirit.

It is our intention that you have come to the awareness that Spirit has been speaking with you, your entire life. We also intend for you to realize how you best prepare for and receive your messages. We encourage you to trust yourself.

You know now how to prepare your outer world in order to receive guidance. This is your relationship to environment. You know what kind of atmosphere to create based on the specific relationship you have with environment. And from this specific scenario, you know the first element of your Intuitive Language—Social (S) or Natural (N).

You know how to prepare your inner world in order to receive guidance. This is your relationship to unconditional love. Based on your specific relationship to unconditional love, you know the emotion or feeling which will bring you closer to an unconditional love state. And from this, you know the second element of your Intuitive Language—Ethereal (E) or Grounded (G).

You know the mode in which you best receive guidance: your clair family. Your primary and secondary clair placed you within a specific clair family. The third element of your Intuitive Language is the name of this family. Explorer. Observer. Conversationalist.

It is our intention, also, that you understand that you can easily train yourself to become multilingual in all of the Intuitive Languages. Simply, you begin by practicing with the neighbouring languages, which have one or more of the same characteristics of your language.

And, finally, you now know the components of living your life in flow and the gifts doing so will give you and all living beings on Earth.

Now it's up to you. Practice daily. Find a community to support your growth. But most of all, have fun!

Part Five

Resources

Glossary of Terms

Clairs—the senses of the intuitive system.

Clairvoyant—one who receives intuitive messages in a visual manner.

Clairaudient—one who receives intuitive messages in an auditory manner.

Clairsomatic—one who receives intuitive messages via physical sensations.

Clairemotive—one who receives intuitive messages via emotions or feelings.

Claircognitive—one who receives intuitive messages as a knowing or thought.

Clairsentient—one who identifies as a clairsomatic, clairemotive, and/or a claircognitive.

Flow—the state of allowing oneself to be in the rhythm of one's own internal energies, the energies of world around them, and the Universal energies.

Glossary of Metaphors

THIS LIST OF METAPHORS IS NOT DEFINITE, NOR IS IT COMPLETE. These are the most common metaphors which appear in my students' meditations, along with the most common translations of these metaphors. If it doesn't resonate with you, let it go. I strongly encourage you to ask yourself, first, what each one means to you. For example, what makes a deer different from a bear?

Balloon: celebration, joy, uplifting

Beach: relaxation, serenity

Bear: protection, hibernation

Bird: freedom, soar (Each specific bird will have their own meaning for you, if you're not sure what that meaning would be, compare the bird you are seeing with another bird; or focus on the colour or size of the bird)

Book: knowledge, wisdom

Boxes: compartmentalization, grouping, containing

Butterflies: transformation, change

Coin: wealth

Dandelions: wishes, healing, nuisance (depends on how you relate to dandelions!)

Deer: graceful, fearful, compassion

Doll: playfulness, childhood

Feathers: message from the angels or loved ones who have transitioned

Flower: growth (specific flower will have its own meaning for you)

Fox: clever, stealthy, playful

Ladder: ascension, rising

Lightbulb: idea, light

Lightening: power, electric, precise energy focus

Moon: feminine, cycles, emotions

Mountains: goals, intentions

Music: harmony, clairaudience

Ocean: Universe, connection to all there is; calm waters = smooth sailing ahead; turbulent waters = danger or proceed with caution

Owl: wisdom, night

Phone: communication

Rabbit: fertility, quick, luck

Rain: cleansing

Rainbow: all aspects of something, harmony, good fortune

River: Flow state, life

Snake: healer, shedding your old self to reveal your new self

Squirrel: resourceful, distraction

Stars: Universe, Oneness

Sun: masculine, energy, power, growth

Tree: wisdom, stability, grounded/rooted (specific tree will have its own meaning for you)

Acknowledgments

Obviously, this book would not have been written without the Tri Luminii! I am deeply grateful for them and our ever-evolving relationship. I have learned so much from the Tri Luminii and continued to be humbled by their choice to communicate to you, through me. Thank you, Tri Luminii, for trusting me with your message. I love you.

I spoke about my love story with Elliott in the Unconditional Love section. I can't imagine traveling this crazy journey of life without him. In the early years of my communication with the Tri Luminii, Elliott and I would begin our days channeling them - listening to their lessons and Elliott would ask them amazing questions which would stretch my ability to trance and the Tri Luminii's ability to find the vocabulary within my mind! He was there when I met the Tri Luminii on our family cruise. He held me in the Cuban waters so that the Tri Luminii could feel what it was like to float in water (all the while, he was being repeatedly nipped at the ankles by the "pesky pescados!"). Elliott wiped away my tears when the Tri Luminii went silent halfway through the writing of this book. He is a talented intuitive in his own right and multilingual in his Intuitive Languages. Elliott is my grounding rock and my soaring eagle in vision. This book never would have been finished without his support and encouragement. I am so deeply grateful for everything we have and continue to create together. Thank you, Elliott, for being a true partner in every aspect of life. I love you.

Becoming a mom has, by far, been the most rewarding role I have ever achieved! When Liam and Ethan arrived in my life, I became a nurturer, advocate, teacher, and student. They are my greatest joy. Elliott and I made the conscious decision to normalize intuition with them from the start. That was easy enough in the early years. As they became school-aged, we held our breath as they ventured out and shined their Light with others. Would they be ridiculed or outcasted? Turns out they found some really great friends along the way who either shared their interest in all things woo, or at least tolerated it! It's so beautiful to witness the ease of manifestation which comes with an intuitive system which was never shut down. When the boys were little, they endured some health challenges. Elliott and I needed to be advocates for their healthcare and stand up to the status quo allopathic approach to medicine. In doing so, we relied heavily on our intuition. It guided us to the right practitioners for each boy and, quite literally, saved their lives. The strength and determination to follow our intuition set the stage for stepping out publicly as an intuitive. Liam and Ethan continue to be an inspiration for me—to show up fully and embrace my woo! Thank you, my sweet boys, for your love, encouragement and continuing to be you! I love you.

Speaking of mothering...I am blessed with a mom who has cheered me on throughout all my different endeavours in life. I have never taken for granted that I always felt I could talk with her about intuition and energy. She never questioned my abilities. In fact, Mom is a strong intuitive and regularly receives visions in dreams. She is my model for a loving, open-minded, and supportive mom. I can only hope my sons feel the unconditional love from me as I have from my mom. She was also instrumental in seeing this book to completion. When I needed a change of scenery, I packed up my laptop and headed to her house on the lake. And, although we are big chatters when we get together, she held herself back and let me write! (And had a glass of wine waiting for when the day's writing was done!) Mom had a bunkie built on top of the boathouse during lockdown. It quickly became my writing retreat. That little piece of heaven helped me work through multiple chapters. Thank you, Mom, for your undying support and unconditional love. I love you.

Each month, I mastermind with a group of ladies who are the sisters I never had. In fact, "sisters" isn't strong enough to describe my love and connection with them. We call ourselves the Faith Keepers. Jill wrote about us in her book, *Loud Woman*. Debby, Jill, and JKC live in the US. Carrie and Clare are in England. I'm in Canada. We met years ago in a business program. We have supported each other in the ups and downs of business and life. We've celebrated, cried, and laughed our way through wins, losses, health challenges, deaths of loved ones, lockdown, and growth. In one of our meetings, back in 2019, I flippantly mentioned the Tri Luminii wanted to write a book with me. Well, needless to say, that was that. The plan for the book was mapped out in that session! Thank you, ladies, for truly being my Faith Keepers. I love you.

One of the Faith Keepers needs a thanks all of her own. Debby is the woman at the helm of Highlander Press. She has been infinitely patient with the Tri Luminii and me as deadlines moved a few times in this process! I panicked when the Tri Luminii went silent halfway through the writing process. She calmed me and helped me focus on what I could do while we waited for them to come back online. Thank you, Debby, for being my guide throughout the publishing process and a true friend! I love you.

Where would a girl be without her friends? Three of my closest friends have held my hand throughout the writing of *Intuitive Languages*. Asha and I started writing our books around the same time. We shared our frustrations, questions, and celebrations. Her beautiful book, *You Are the Medicine*, is already out in the world and is a best seller. Christine was ready for a good belly laugh and meal whenever I needed to stop taking myself so seriously! Spending time with her always fills my cup (and wine glass!) and I deeply cherish our time together. Becca and I started out as accountability buddies but quickly became close friends. Our calls, especially during lockdowns, have been balm for my soul. Thank you, ladies, for being true soul sisters to me. I love you.

It is a blessing to be able to make a living doing what you love. It's a double blessing when the people you work with become family. This is my life with my FLOW members. They are a beautiful group of souls who allow me the privilege of stretching them into their full intuitive potential. My first sharing of the Tri Luminii, outside of my immediate family, was with them. Ever since our first monthly chat with the Tri Luminii, this circle within FLOW continues to be the most well-attended. Thank you, FLOW family, for trusting me with your intuitive development and for embracing the Tri Luminii. I love you.

FLOW, the Tri Luminii trancings, *Intuitive Languages*, wouldn't be here today if I hadn't said yes to my own formal intuitive training. I am eternally grateful to Miriam and our amazing group of budding intuitives who met weekly at Miriam's home. Miriam, you stretched me well-beyond what I thought I could do with my intuition. You held the vision of where I would go with this and didn't let me shy away from it! Thank you, Miriam, for answering the call from your guides to be our teacher. I love you.

I opened this book talking about the beautiful cover art and my experience in working with the incredibly talented, Jenny Giles. It was important to me to have a cover which represented the every day dance we all have with the Universe. My intention is you will use it to find your own messages. Thank you, Jenny, for bringing this to life. I love you.

It's a big feat to write a book, but if no one sees it, it won't have the impact I intended! I am grateful for the support we've received from our Kickstarter backers and our launch partners. Thank you for believing in this book and for supporting it. I love you.

Getting the message "out there" is no small task! I am so grateful to have two very special woman working with me who happen to be marketing geniuses. Jill Celeste and Suzanne Tregenza Moore, you ladies are superheroes! Thank you for everything you do. I love you.

Lastly, but certainly not least, I am deeply grateful for YOU! Thank you for choosing to learn about, and grow, your Intuitive Language. Each person who chooses to live their life in intuitive alignment brings us closer to creating a world which functions on an operating system of Unconditional Love. Thank you for being a part of this movement. I love you.

About the Author

Nicole Meltzer, founder of the transformative program Flow, has helped thousands of people tap into and trust their intuition through her international intuitive circles, programs, and presentations. Nicole's lust for travel, art, languages, and architecture have her seeking bridges—both physically and metaphorically—to connect with others. She lives with her soulmate of many lifetimes, Elliott, and their two highly intuitive sons in Newmarket, Ontario, Canada, where the artsy vibe blends with sporty spice.

 instagram.com/meltzernicole
 facebook.com/TriLuminiiwithNicoleMeltzer

About the Publisher

Highlander Press, founded in 2019, is a mid-sized publishing company committed to diversity and sharing big ideas thereby changing the world through words.

Highlander Press guides authors from where they are in the writing-editing-publishing process to where they have an impactful book of which they are proud, making a long-time dream come true. Having authored a book improves your confidence, helps create clarity, and ensures that you claim your expertise.

What makes Highlander Press unique is that their business model focuses on building strong collaborative relationships with other women-owned businesses, which specialize in some aspect of the publishing industry, such as graphic design, book marketing, book launching, copyrights, and publicity. The mantra "a rising tide lifts all boats" is one they embrace.

 facebook.com/highlanderpress

 instagram.com/highlanderpress

 linkedin.com/in/highlanderpress

Printed in Great Britain
by Amazon

17998344R00088